PERSONALITIES
AND POWERS

SIR LEWIS NAMIER

Personalities
and
Powers

GREENWOOD PRESS, PUBLISHERS
WESTPORT, CONNECTICUT

Library of Congress Cataloging in Publication Data

Namier, Sir Lewis Bernstein, 1888-1960.
   Personalities and powers.

   Reprint of the 1955 ed. published by H. Hamilton,
London.
   1. History, Modern--Addresses, essays, lectures.
I. Title.
[D210.N32 1974]   901.9'3   73-20878
ISBN 0-8371-5780-3

First published in Great Britain in 1955 by
Hamish Hamilton, London

Reprinted with the permission of Hamish Hamilton Ltd.

Reprinted in 1974 by Greenwood Press,
a division of Williamhouse-Regency Inc.

Library of Congress Catalog Card Number 73-20878

ISBN 0-8371-5780-3

Printed in the United States of America

CONTENTS

ACKNOWLEDGEMENTS

MY DUTIFUL thanks are due in the first place for permission to make extensive use of material contained in the Royal Archives at Windsor Castle in my essay on King George III. I further wish to thank Mr. Humphrey FitzRoy Newdegate for access to his collection of family papers which have supplied basic material for the essay on 'Country Gentlemen in Parliament, 1750–84'.

Incidental reference to many other collections of manuscripts, which I have examined in connexion with other work, is made in these two essays and in my Romanes Lecture. I wish to express my gratitude to their respective owners.

I am indebted to Dr. M. J. Mannheim for helping me with his expert advice on certain psychological problems.

My thanks are due to the Delegates of the Clarendon Press for permission to reprint my Romanes Lecture, and to London University for permission to reprint my Creighton Lecture.

I have to thank the editors and owners of the periodicals in which various essays originally appeared for permission to reprint them: *History Today* (Essays 2, 4, 5, and 7), *The Listener* (1, 11, and 12), *The New Statesman and Nation* (6), *The Times Literary Supplement* (8), and *World Politics* (10).

L. B. NAMIER

60 *The Grampians, London, W.*6
20 *December* 1954

HUMAN NATURE IN POLITICS

THE TITLE of this essay reproduces that of a famous book published nearly fifty years ago: *Human Nature in Politics*, by Graham Wallas. Its first sentence read: 'The study of politics is just now (1908) in a curiously unsatisfactory position.' 'The thinkers of the past', he wrote, 'from Plato to Bentham and Mill, had each his own view of human nature, and they made those views the basis of their speculations on government'; but he complained that his own contemporaries no longer prefaced their treatises on political science by a definition of human nature, and indeed, he found it difficult to discover whether they possessed any conception of it at all.

Not that he commended the naive, dogmatic definitions supplied by earlier writers: for instance, by the Utilitarians who thought they had found the key to man's behaviour in the hedonistic principle of his seeking pleasure and shunning pain, or by the classical economists with their *homo oeconomicus* desirous to obtain additional wealth with the least sacrifice — systems based on the assumption of man's essential rationality. 'When we see the actions of a man', wrote Macaulay in 1829, 'we know with certainty what he thinks his interest to be'. It was thus assumed that man always acts on a valid, reasonable inference of how best to achieve a preconceived end. Graham Wallas's own conclusion about human nature in politics was that 'most of the political opinions of most men are the result, not of reasoning tested by experience, but of unconscious or half-conscious inference fixed by habit'; and he exhorted students of politics to fight against the tendency to 'exaggerate the intellectuality of mankind'.

Graham Wallas's criticism of the *homo sapiens* in politics won an easy victory; the time was ripe for his thrust, and the silence of writers about human nature in politics, of which he complained, may have been a dim, uneasy precognition of his analysis. By now we have travelled a great deal further along Graham Wallas's path. For him atavistic memories and mental habits formed the stock material of man's unconscious thinking. Since then we have learnt about fixations in both individuals and groups, about psychological displacements and projections, and the externalization of unresolved inner conflicts. A man's relation, for instance, to his father or to his nurse may determine the pattern of his later political conduct or of his intellectual preoccupations without his being in the least conscious of the connexion; and self-deception concerning the origin and character of his seemingly intellectual tenets enables him to deceive others: the intensity of his hidden passion sharpens his mental faculties and may even create the appearances of cold, clear-sighted objectivity. I remember how many years ago, when a perfect case in support of a political thesis was presented to a very wise friend of mine, he replied: 'I should be convinced by the argument if I did not know the passion which is behind it.' He was right to be cautious though he did not apprehend the source of that passion; yet even the recognition of it does not necessarily prove that the thesis was wrong. Or to take a historical example: a sentence in Talleyrand's *Memoirs*, seemingly unrelated to politics, in a flash illumines one aspect of his political conduct. He writes: 'I say in order to have said it once, and hoping never to think of it again, that I am perhaps the only man of distinguished birth...who has not for a single week of his life known the joy of staying under his parental roof.' Here was bitterness which he, writing at the age of over sixty, wished he could overcome. Neglected by his parents and brought up by dependents who extolled to him the greatness of his family, he went through life a very conscious *grand seigneur* who associated by preference with inferiors and, devoid of any feeling for his own class—its primary representatives were to him his parents—contributed with cold indifference to its downfall.

Examples of this kind, positive and negative, to be found in the life of any man, make us less prone to accept at face value interpretations of beliefs, principles, and actions, even if given in all sincerity. Unconscious promptings combine with rational thought, and in every action there are inscrutable components. Undoubtedly one of the most important lines of advance for history, and especially for biography, will be through a knowledge of modern psychology. Still, care is required in applying it. The unqualified practitioner must not be let loose, not even on the dead, and a mere smattering of psychology is likely to result in superficial, hasty judgements framed in a nauseating jargon. But even to the expert, available psychological data yield at best a fragmentary picture. Lastly, there is pragmatic validity in conscious thought unaffected by psychological origins; and action, however prompted, speaks its own language of unmistakable reality. Although we know that man's actions are mostly conditioned by factors other than reason, in practice we have to assume their rational character until the contrary has been specifically established; and when dealing with the mysteries of the human mind, we had best say with the preacher: 'And now, brethren, let us boldly face the difficulty, and then pass it over.' Yet awareness of the vast depths, unprobed and largely unfathomable, enjoins on us both humility and caution in approaching the problem of human nature in politics.

Even worse than our position with regard to the psychology of individuals, the politicians, is that regarding groups, the masses, the crowd in action. We are as yet merely groping for an approach to mass psychology: some of the positive chapters of Graham Wallas's book now strike one as almost as naive as the beliefs he effectively destroyed. We do not even know some of the means whereby men communicate thoughts or emotions to each other. I remember a remark which in 1911 I heard from Sir Reginald Wingate: he said that after all the years in the Sudan it remained a mystery for him how news travelled among the natives—even heliographs would not have enabled them to transmit it with that speed. *La grande peur*, the panic which seized the French countryside in July 1789 and consolidated the Great Revolution, is the outstanding example of a nation-wide psychological upheaval; but smaller tremors of that kind can be traced in almost every revolution. Besides, there is what in current terminology would be described as the 'intellectual climate', dimly communicated and developed by some kind of unconscious telepathy, which seems to affect the great mass of the population.

Very seldom do we come across in history powerful political movements, such as the revolution of 1688, planned and executed with a clear purpose: this was a rising of politically conscious men against the civil and spiritual tyranny of the Stuarts. In most cases the essence of political mass movements is shrouded in darkness. It is hard to believe that on the Paris barricades men died in 1830 in order to preserve the Charter, or in February 1848 in order to obtain an extension of the franchise; more probably behind these two risings were much the same forces as behind that of June 1848, described by Alexis de Tocqueville as the greatest and most singular insurrection in French history. And singular it certainly was, in that 100,000 insurgents fought with remarkable skill and cohesion, though, to quote Tocqueville once more, 'without a war-cry, without chiefs, or a standard'; or in simpler terms: without intellectuals having stamped their doctrines or ideas on the rising. George Meredith calls it an ironical habit of mind to believe that the wishes of men are expressed by their utterances; even more ironical, or naive, would it be to judge of the essence of mass movements by the pronouncements or professions of those who manage to filch them. So far we have hardly reached the fringes of the field of mass psychology, the most basic factor in history. All we can do is to try faithfully to state discernible facts, pose problems, but be chary of drawing conclusions.

One inevitable result of heightened psychological awareness is, however, a change of attitude towards so-called political ideas. To treat them as the offspring of pure reason would be to assign to them a parentage about as mythological as that of Pallas Athene. What matters most is the underlying emotions, the music, to which ideas are a mere libretto, often of very inferior quality; and once the emotions have ebbed, the ideas, established high and dry, become doctrine, or at best innocuous *clichés.* Even the principles of the Glorious Revolution, after victory had been irrevocably won and they had changed into an accepted profession of faith, came to sound somewhat hollow. I have been blamed by a very friendly and appreciative critic of my work for taking the mind out of history, for discerning self-interest or ambition in men, but showing insufficient appreciation of political principles and of abstract ideals to which their votaries try to make reality conform. That criticism is so relevant to the subject of this essay that I propose to make it the text of what I have still to say.

To start with taking the mind out of history. It certainly seems impossible to attach to conscious political thought the importance which was ascribed to it a hundred, or even fifty, years ago. History is primarily, and to a growing extent, made by man's mind and nature; but his mind does not work with the rationality that was once deemed its noblest attribute— which does not, however, mean that it necessarily works any worse. Strictly logical conclusions based on insufficient data are a deadly danger, especially when pride is taken in the performance; and our data in politics are necessarily exiguous and fragmentary. Even within that range, the facts we can at any time consciously muster and master in a quasi-scientific manner are a mere fraction of what is present in our subconscious mind. The less, therefore, man clogs the free play of his mind with political doctrine and dogma, the better for his thinking. And the irrational is not necessarily unreasonable: it may only be that we cannot explain it, or that we misinterpret it, in terms of our conscious thought. An absurd proof does not necessarily invalidate a contention: wrong labels are sometimes stuck on produce of unknown provenance.

I came across a striking case of that kind some forty years ago, when working at Yale on the correspondence of Ezra Stiles, an eighteenth-century president of the college. A New England doctor reported to him exciting news: he had discovered that the Red Indians were of Mongol extraction; but being that day in a hurry, he was going to produce his evidence in his next letter. This was indeed exciting—it reminded me of the story of Fermat's famous mathematical theorem; so I went in search of that next letter; but as the papers were not properly arranged and indexed, it took me some time to trace it. When I did, this I found was his evidence: Noah had three sons, Japhet, Shem, and Ham, and wherever we go we find that the descendants of Ham serve those of Japhet; but the Red Indians had no Negro slaves: hence they must be descended from Shem. Funny, isn't it? In time I have come to think differently. The doctor, a trained observer, must unconsciously have based his conclusion on similarly unconscious observations; but being a New England Puritan, he sought and found his evidence in the Old Testament. Every age and every country has a cherished lore and will draw on it in season and out of season; and political principles are often as irrelevant as the argument of the doctor.

As for human motives: tell a story without attributing any, and they will be readily supplied by others from the common stock. The 'economic motive' of the Victorians and the 'will to power' of the Germans are current coin, and acquisitive instincts or ambition offer plausible explanations of human actions, which can be contrasted with the unselfish pursuit of ideals. But is there such a clear division in the depths of the human mind and nature? Fear, conscious or unconscious, is often the impelling force behind money-making, over-eating, intellectual pursuits, or endeavours to benefit humanity. And even behind money-making there may be a creative urge or thought for the community. On the other hand, is there no ambition, and no *hubris*, in the man who tries to make reality conform to his so-called ideals? To react against cruelty, injustice, or oppression is one thing; to have a nostrum for securing man's freedom or his happiness is a very different matter. And 'idealism' or 'idealist' are misnomers when bestowed merely because self-interest or ambition is not writ large on the surface.

I remember a story from that admirable book, *The Ladies of Alderley*. In September 1841 Mrs. Stanley, in a letter to her mother-in-law, expressed her dislike for a house because it was 'very romantic'. 'I *don't* understand' wrote back Lady Stanley 'why you should wish it not to be *very romantic*.' Mrs. Stanley replied: 'When I said romantic I meant damp.' Probably it was not merely creepers and thatched roofs which made these terms synonymous for her: the affinity of sound between 'romantic' and 'rheumatic' may have played its part. So it does in the frequent confusion between an 'ideologue' and an 'idealist'. And what shams and disasters political ideologies are apt to be, we surely have had opportunity to learn. Never have the popular masses been worse enslaved than under what calls itself 'the dictatorship of the proletariate', nor has ever worse scum wielded power than under the Nazi régime proclaiming 'the rule of the *élite*'. But even far less cruel or fierce political ideologies have played havoc with human welfare. There is a fixity in them that makes them outlive even the few factors to which they were originally correlated; which is the reason why radicals who rely on systems so often produce mere junk—*des vieilleries: ils ne changent pas leur baggage*—they do not repack their ideological baggage. Moreover, almost all ideologies vastly overrate man's capacity to foresee the consequences and repercussions of ideals forced on reality.

Some political philosophers complain of 'a tired lull' and the absence at present of argument on general politics in this country: practical solutions are sought for concrete problems, while programmes and ideals are forgotten by both parties. But to me this attitude seems to betoken a greater national maturity, and I can only wish that it may long continue undisturbed by the workings of political philosophy.

2

THE PROFESSION OF HISTORIAN

MARC BLOCH describes his book, *The Historian's Craft*, as 'the memorandum of a craftsman who has always liked to reflect over his daily task', and names as its primary aim 'to explain how and why a historian practises his trade'. But the 'why' of our interest in history comes first; and the answer might perhaps be summed up in a Leonardian 'thus nature has made us'. Our civilization, unlike some others, has always been historically-minded, both in its classical and in its Christian heritage: the Greeks and Romans were history-writing peoples; and Christianity 'is essentially a historical religion ... the beginnings of the faith are also its foundations'.

We try to understand; and the self-intelligibility even of the present is a myth:

> A society that could be completely moulded by its immediately preceding period would have to have a structure so malleable as to be virtually invertebrate.

There is also 'entertainment value' in history: it appeals to large numbers of readers. Men in society are its subject; and 'the spectacle of human activity ... is ... designed to seduce the imagination ... above all when ... adorned with the subtle enchantment of the unfamiliar'—what Leibniz called 'the thrill of learning singular things'. Lastly, experience shows 'that it is impossible to decide in advance whether even the most abstract speculations may not eventually prove extraordinarily helpful in practice'. This sounds apologetic: in fact, the French title of the book (of which only the second limb is reproduced in the

8

English translation) reads: *Apologie pour l'Histoire, ou Métier d'Historien*. But then Cournot writes, and Bloch seems to endorse his dicta, about 'the scant popularity' which history enjoys in France and 'the under-developed consciousness of the historical tradition' among the French lower classes: the French people in the mass being 'everlastingly inclined to reconstruct the world on lines of reason'. And yet, one might object, there is hardly a nation whose political life has been so much haunted as that of the French by historical memories resulting in obsessionist repetition. Perhaps disparagement of historical lore and the appeal to reason are with them an ineffective bid for freedom.

Even where not on the defensive, historians have been afflicted by hesitancies and searchings of soul, especially when, on a wrong analogy with the exact sciences, they went in search of absolute certainties and universal laws such as cannot be formulated about human actions. This made some of them draw untenable distinctions between mere events of an accidental character, which, they thought, could be left out of account, and the great course of history accessible to rational analysis and comprehension; while others, humiliated and disillusioned by failure to achieve the unattainable, resigned themselves to treating history as a mental exercise in which questions may be asked but had better be left unanswered. Now, with a change of mental climate in science itself, 'we find it far easier to regard certainty and universality as questions of degree', and to assess more soberly what history can be expected to achieve, and by what means.

History is 'the most difficult of all the sciences', because of its enormous range and the variety of phenomena it covers, and because of the inherent difficulties of its technique. It starts wherever human action sets in, and there are hardly any limits to its auxiliary disciplines, except those set by the capacities of the individual historian. Further, as all the data of history are specific, 'a historical phenomenon can never be understood apart from its moment in time'. For the atomic scientist the time it takes for a radioactive substance to change is a fundamental datum, but it is bound to no one moment or period: it is unplaced in time; whereas 'historical time is a concrete and living reality with an irreversible onward rush'. Historical events cannot be experimentally reproduced; and knowledge of human activities is 'a knowledge of their tracks'—of marks 'perceptible to the senses, which some phenomenon, in itself inaccessible, has left behind'. The 'sense of virtually unlimited progress, granted to a science like chemistry ... is refused to us'. We can only know what the past, consciously or otherwise, has yielded to us. Still, historical technique is advancing. There was a time when the chief reliance was on intentional evidence: accounts written for posterity. But gradually 'historical research has been led to place more and more confidence ... in the evidence of witnesses in spite of themselves'; incidental evidence and unconscious confessions are more likely to be unvitiated by deliberate purpose (though even they call for psychological scrutiny).

> Despite our inevitable subordination to the past, we have freed ourselves at least to the extent that, eternally condemned to know only by means of its 'tracks', we are nevertheless successful in knowing far more of the past than the past itself had thought good to tell us. Properly speaking, it is a glorious victory of mind over its material.

But 'texts ... speak only when they are properly questioned'; 'every historical research supposes that the inquiry has a direction ... there must be a guiding spirit': 'the method of cross-examination must be very elastic ... yet be able ... to act as a magnet drawing findings out of the document'. 'In the last analysis it is human consciousness which is the subject-matter of history'; 'historical facts are, in essence, psychological facts'; and by now we have learnt to look out for the deeper undercurrent of thought and emotion, and to 'overhear what was never intended to be said'.

Typically French are Bloch's subtle observations on the language of history.

> ... each science has its appropriate aesthetics of language. Human actions are essentially very delicate phenomena. ... Properly to translate them into words and, hence, to fathom them rightly

(for can anyone perfectly understand what he does not know how to express?), great delicacy of language and precise shadings of verbal tone are necessary.

Or again:

> ... the first tool needed by any analysis is an appropriate language; a language capable of describing the precise outlines of the facts, while preserving the necessary flexibility to adapt itself to further discoveries and, above all, a language which is neither vacillating nor ambiguous.

But for history 'the day of precision has not yet arrived'—'why ... is it so slow in coming?'

> Chemistry has fashioned its own supply of symbols and even its own words.... This is because chemistry had the great advantage of being applied to realities which were, by their very nature, incapable of naming themselves... whether we call it vitriol or sulphuric acid, the substance itself has not influenced the choice. It is quite otherwise with a science of humanity. Men gave names to their actions, their beliefs, and the various aspects of their social life without waiting until they became objects of disinterested research. Hence, history receives its vocabulary, for the most part, from the very subject-matter. It accepts it, already worn out and deformed by long usage; frequently, moreover, ambiguous from the very beginning....

How many different meanings are attached to 'capitalism'! What date should be assigned to its appearance? 'There are as many birth-certificates as there are historians.' They obviously talk of different things. But a word-symbol misapplied is apt to result in anachronism: 'the most unpardonable of sins in a time-science'.

There are many other memorable discourses in this small, unfinished book, from which the two last chapters, on 'Explanation in History' and 'The Problem of Prevision', are missing. These, writes Lucien Febvre, one of Bloch's closest friends and collaborators, would perhaps 'have been the most strictly original of the whole'. Marc Bloch, of Alsatian Jewish origin, was one of the foremost French medievalists, and Professor at the Sorbonne. A veteran of the First War, he was recalled to the colours at the age of fifty-three in 1939. After the collapse, writes Febvre, he could have fled to the U.S. 'But he refused to leave France, even the France of Vichy'. And then, to quote Bloch's own words, this book was 'begun as a simple antidote by which, amid sorrows and anxieties both personal and collective', he sought 'a little peace of mind'. It is his testament as a historian. He was a leading member of the Resistance; was captured by the Germans in the spring of 1944, atrociously tortured, and finally executed. Somewhere in the book Bloch speaks of 'civilizations of people who are not civilized'.

3

MONARCHY AND THE PARTY SYSTEM

(Romanes Lecture, 1952)

I HAVE chosen for my subject a story with a happy ending, with a striking dénouement, unforeseen and unpredictable while it was shaping. Constitutional monarchy—the union of a hereditary Crown with parliamentary government—is, to quote Mr. Churchill, 'of all the institutions which have grown up among us over the centuries ... the most deeply founded and dearly cherished'.[1] British monarchy detached from British politics has become the link of the Commonwealth of Nations, and the pivot of government in a number of co-ordinated countries; it is seen to secure basic continuity in government with a variability unequalled under any other system. But in the earlier stages the growth of constitutional monarchy was impeded rather than aided by conscious political thought—the 'odious title' of Prime Minister was decried, and the extinction of party prayed for. Even now constitutional monarchy, though anchored both in the thought and affection of the nation, depends for its smooth working on the continuance of concrete factors by which it was moulded. Hence the importance of discerning them.

What are the basic elements of constitutional monarchy? A Sovereign placed above parties and politics; a Prime Minister and Government taking rise from Parliament, and received rather than designated by the Sovereign, yet as 'H.M. confi-

[1] In the broadcast delivered on 7 February 1952, after the death of King George VI.

13

dential servants' deriving from the Royal Prerogative that essential executive character which an elected legislature could not impart to them; and an unpolitical Civil Service whose primary connexion is with the Crown, and which, while subordinated to party-governments, is unaffected by their changes: the two permanent elements, the Crown and the Civil Service, which not by chance together left the political arena, supply the framework for the free play of parliamentary politics and governments. Under royal government the sovereign was the undisputed, immediate head of the executive; under parliamentary government, it is the prime minister; but no clear-cut formula is possible for the intervening period of 'mixed government', during which the direction of government gradually passed from the sovereign to the prime minister by a process that can be logically defined but eludes precise dating. The prime minister replaced the sovereign as actual head of the executive when the choice of the prime minister no longer lay with the sovereign; the sovereign lost the choice when strongly organized, disciplined parliamentary parties came into existence; and party discipline depends primarily on the degree to which the member depends on the party for his seat. The sovereign can keep clear of party-politics only so long as it is not incumbent on him or her to choose the prime minister. Thus constitutional monarchy as now understood hinges to a high degree on the working of the modern party system.

In 1761 not one parliamentary election was determined by party, and in 1951 not one constituency returned a non-party member. To trace how that change has come about will require a most thorough knowledge of constituencies and elections, of members and parliaments, and of constitutional ideas and realities throughout the formative period: to acquire that knowledge is one of the tasks of the History of Parliament on which we are now engaged, and can only be accomplished by a great collective effort. In this lecture I propose to set before you tentative outlines: suggestions rather than conclusions. I shall deal mainly with the earlier period covered by my own research; still, in a broad survey I am bound to travel beyond its limits, and I have drawn on the help and advice most generously accorded by fellow workers in our field.[1]

2

The king's business in parliament had at all times to be transacted through ministers; and as parliament grew in importance, so did the minister capable of managing it. Yet under 'mixed government' even for the securing of parliamentary support royal favour and confidence were needed, and as late as 1786, Robert Beatson, in his *Political Index* dedicated to Adam Smith, placed the names of the leading ministers under the heading 'A List of Prime Ministers and Favourites, from the accession of King Henry VIII to the present time'. The personal element inevitably determined the exact relation between the sovereign and his advisers, and at all times there were kings who yielded easy assent to ministers or deferred to the guidance of favourites; and few more so than George III, especially in the first decade of his reign. Horace Walpole, accurately informed by his friend H. S. Conway, wrote in 1769 that George III 'never interfered with his Ministers', but 'seemed to resign himself entirely to their conduct for the time' —a statement borne out by the king's voluminous correspondence wherein, as a rule, he repeats with approval advice tendered by his ministers. He would become active only when, in Walpole's words, 'he was to undo an administration'.[2] Still, 'the King's independency', that is, his right to choose and dismiss ministers, was a constitutional axiom; and however hard

---

[1] We are working on the history of parliament as a team interchanging ideas and information; but here I name only those who have either given me unprinted work to read or who have directly contributed suggestions bearing on my theme, or quotations illustrating my points. For such help I am indebted to Professor A. Aspinall, Mr. Asa Briggs, Mr. M. G. Brock, Mr. I. R. Christie, Mr. Kitson Clark, Professor Norman Gash, Mr. David Gray, Dr. R. W. Greaves, Mr. J. B. Owen, Dr. J. H. Plumb, Mr. R. R. Sedgwick, Miss L. S. Sutherland, Miss Joan Wake, and Professor Robert Walcott.

[2] Horace Walpole, *Memoirs of the Reign of King George III*, ed. G. F. R. Barker, vol. iii, p. 66.

politicians strove for office, they would, each and all, declare their extreme reluctance to enter or retain it unless assured of the king's favour willingly accorded. Newcastle in 1759 voiced 'the most ardent wishes' for the Prince of Wales to succeed 'in such a situation as shall leave his hands free . . . to form his plan of government with advantage';[1] George Grenville claimed to have 'entered into the King's service . . . to hinder the law from being indecently and unconstitutionally given to him' — 'to prevent any undue and unwarrantable force being put upon the Crown';[2] and Pitt repeatedly declared that he would not be forced upon the king by parliament, nor come into his service against his consent. When the Fox–North Coalition had succeeded in imposing themselves on the king driven to the brink of abdication, Fox, who treated Whig 'anti-monarchism as the main principle of the British Constitution'[3] addressed him, on 16 April 1783, in the following terms:[4]

> Mr. Fox hopes that Your Majesty will not think him presumptuous or improperly intruding upon Your Majesty with professions, if he begs leave most humbly to implore Your Majesty to believe that both the Duke of Portland and he have nothing so much at heart as to conduct Your Majesty's affairs, both with respect to measures and to persons, in the manner that may give Your Majesty the most satisfaction, and that, whenever Your Majesty will be graciously pleased to condescend even to hint your inclinations upon any subject, that it will be the study of Your Majesty's Ministers to show how truly sensible they are of Your Majesty's goodness.

During the next forty years parties were gradually shaping in parliament, but they did not as yet dominate it, and in theory relations between king and ministers remained unchanged. 'If you do not like us why do you not turn us out?', asked the

---

[1] Add. MS. 32889, ff. 136–7; quoted in my book, *England in the Age of the American Revolution*, pp. 113–14.

[2] *Grenville Papers*, vol. ii, pp. 86 and 106.

[3] R. Pares, 'George III and the Politicians', *Transactions of the R. Hist. Soc.*, 5th series, vol. i (1951), p. 128.

[4] *Correspondence of King George III*, ed. Sir John Fortescue, vol. vi, p. 357, no. 4308.

Duke of Wellington of George IV in July 1821.[1] And in March 1827 Stephen Lushington, M.P., Secretary of the Treasury, still attributed to the king the absolute and unqualified choice of his ministers;[2] while Canning, in language curiously reminiscent of that held by Bute sixty-five years earlier, inveighed against aristocratic 'confederacies', and discoursed on 'the real vigour of the Crown when it chooses to put forth its own strength'.[3]

When in 1834 William IV had dismissed the Melbourne Government, Peel claimed a 'fair trial' for the ministers of the king's choice; and its semblance was conceded by the Whigs who, having won the ensuing general election, refrained from a direct vote of censure on the Address.[4] As late as 1846, Wellington and Peel, at variance with a majority of their party, harped on their position and duties as Ministers of the Crown and declared that, were they to stand alone, they would still have 'to enable Her Majesty to meet her Parliament and to carry on the business of the country'.

> I was of the opinion [declared Wellington] that the formation of a Government in which Her Majesty would have confidence, was of much greater importance than the opinions of any individual on the Corn Laws, or any other law....

And Peel, whose ideas of an independent executive similarly seemed to hark back to the earlier period, thus attempted to define his position:

> I see it over and over again repeated, that I am under a personal obligation for holding the great office which I have the honour to occupy... that I was placed in that position by a

---

[1] *The Diary of Henry Hobhouse (1820–7)* ed. A. Aspinall, p. 67; see also *The Journal of Mrs. Arbuthnot*, 27 June 1821, ed. F. Bamford and the Duke of Wellington, vol. i, p. 103.

[2] S. R. Lushington to Sir Wm. Knighton, 26 March 1827: *Letters of King George IV*, ed. A. Aspinall, vol. iii, pp. 207–10.

[3] G. Canning to J. W. Croker, 3 April 1827: *The Croker Papers*, ed. L. J. Jennings, vol. i, p. 368.

[4] See G. Kitson Clark, *Peel and the Conservative Party. A Study in Politics, 1832–41*, pp. 211–12, and 237–8.

C

party.... I am not under an obligation to any man, or to any body of men, for being compelled ... to undergo the official duties and labour which I have undertaken....

And next:

I have served four Sovereigns.... I served each of those Sovereigns at critical times and in critical circumstances ... and ... there was but ... one reward which I desired ... namely, the simple acknowledgment, on their part, that I had been to them a loyal and faithful Minister....

To this Disraeli retorted that the queen would never have called on Peel in 1841 had he not 'placed himself, as he said, at the head of the Gentlemen of England'.

I say [continued Disraeli] it is utterly impossible to carry on your Parliamentary Constitution except by political parties. I say there must be distinct principles as lines of conduct adopted by public men....

Above all, maintain the line of demarcation between parties; for it is only by maintaining the independence of party that you can maintain the integrity of public men, and the power and influence of Parliament itself.[1]

Here then were two conceptions of the ministers' relations to Crown and Party: one reflecting the past but still adducible without patent absurdity; the other, much more in harmony with the realities which then were shaping, and which, once shaped, were soon to be mistaken for primordial elements of the British Constitution. The past and the future, capable of neat definition, impinged on a period of mixed character, first, by a theoretical carry over, and next, by historical antedating. As a result, 'by a double distortion', to quote Mr. Sedgwick's summing up, George III 'has been represented as having endeavoured to imitate the Stuarts when he ought to have anticipated Queen Victoria'.[2]

---

[1] Hansard, vol. lxxxiii, 3rd series, 22 January 1846, cols. 92–3, 120, and 123.

[2] *Letters from George III to Lord Bute, 1756–1766*, ed. Romney Sedgwick, Introduction, p. viii.

3

According to contemporaries the complex system of the 'mixed form of government' combined 'by skilful division of power' the best of the monarchy, aristocracy, and democracy; and it was viewed by them with pride and satisfaction. Mechanically minded and with a bent towards the ingenious, they relished its 'checks and controls', and the 'mutual watchfulness and jealousy' which its delicate balance demanded from all concerned; and they cherished a constitution which safeguarded their rights and freedoms when 'in almost every other nation of Europe' public liberty was 'extremely upon the decline'.[1] George III, that much maligned monarch, was truly representative when, abhorring both 'despotism' and 'anarchy', he extolled 'the beauty, excellence, and perfection of the British constitution as by law established'.[2] What was bound to escape contemporaries was the insoluble contradictions of a political system which, incongruously, associated a royal executive with parliamentary struggles for office. Yet the two had to coexist in an organic transition from royal to parliamentary government.

A parliamentary régime is based on the unhindered alternating of party-governments. But while contending party leaders can in turn fill the office of prime minister, how could the king freely pass from the one side to the other, and in turn captain opposite teams? It was far more consonant with his position to try to heal 'the unhappy divisions that subsist between men' and form an administration from 'the best of all parties' than to quit 'one set of men for another'. Could he give up with unconcern the ministers whom he had chosen and upheld, and in whose actions and policy he had participated? In 1779 it was but natural for him to stipulate that on a change of government past measures should 'be treated with proper respect' and that 'no blame be laid' on them. And here is a naive but sincere statement of his position: 'I have no wish but for the prosperity

[1] David Hume, *Essays Moral, Political, and Literary* (1742).
[2] *Correspondence of King George III*, vol. iv, pp. 220-1, no. 2451; the King to Lord North, 14 November 1778.

of my Dominions therefore must look on all who will not heartily assist me as bad men as well as ungrateful subjects.' And on another occasion: '... whilst I have no wish but for the good and prosperity of my country, it is impossible that the nation shall not stand by me; if they will not, they shall have another King.'[1] He did not think in terms of parties; but their existence prevented the king, while he remained the actual head of the executive, from leading an undivided nation.

Yet it was impossible to eliminate party from parliament: an assembly whose leaders contend for office and power was bound to split into factions divided by personal animosities and trying to preserve their identity and coherence in and out of office. Consequently when in office they laid themselves open to the accusation of monopolizing power and of 'keeping the King in fetters'; in opposition, of distressing the government with intention to 'storm the Closet' and force themselves, unconstitutionally, on the king. No consistent defence of parties was possible under the 'mixed form of government', and this undoubtedly retarded their development and consolidation. To Bolingbroke parties when based on a 'difference of principles and designs' were 'misfortune enough', but if continued without it an even greater misfortune, for then they were mere 'instruments of private ambition'.[2] David Hume denounced them as subversive of government and begetting 'the fiercest animosities' among fellow citizens; but he next conceded that to 'abolish all distinctions of party may not be practicable, perhaps not desirable, in a free government'.[3] Burke squarely contended that party-divisions were, for good or evil, 'things inseparable from free government'; and in his well-known eulogy of party as a union of men endeavouring to promote the

[1] *Correspondence of King George III*, ed. Sir John Fortescue, vol. i, p. 375, no. 353, the King to Pitt, 15 July 1766; vol. iv, p. 517, no. 3875, the King to the Lord Chancellor, 11 December 1779; vol. iv, p. 507, no. 2865, same to same, 3 December 1779; vol. vi, p. 151, no. 3973, the King to Lord North, 4 November 1782; vol. iv, p. 65, no. 2230, same to same, 17 March 1778.

[2] *A Dissertation upon Parties* (1734).

[3] op. cit., part I, essay VII, 'Of Parties in General', and part II, essay XIV, 'Of the Coalition of Parties'.

national interest on a common principle, gave a forecast of parliamentary government. Men so connected, he wrote, must strive 'to carry their common plan into execution with all the power and authority of the State'; in forming an administration give 'their party preference in all things'; and not 'accept any offers of power in which the whole body is not included'.[1] While professing adherence to the Revolution Settlement, by implication he eliminated the rights of the Crown, and obliquely argued that in fact the royal executive had ceased to exist, replaced by the monstrous contraption of a cabal set on separating 'the Court from Administration'. The 'double Cabinet', a product of Burke's fertile, disordered, and malignant imagination, long bedevilled his own party and their spiritual descendants.

That the House of Commons might ultimately 'engross the whole power of the constitution', wresting the executive from the Crown, was apprehended by Hume. How then could they be 'confined within the proper limits'?

> I answer [wrote Hume] that the interest of the body is here restrained by that of the individuals. . . . The Crown has so many offices at its disposal, that, when assisted by the honest and disinterested part of the House, it will always command the resolutions of the whole so far, at least, as to preserve the antient constitution from danger.

He thus discerned within the House itself the main obstacle to parliamentary government: a majority of its members were as yet by their ideas, interests, and pursuits, unfitted for a system of party politics.

4

Parliamentary struggles for office necessarily produce a dichotomy of 'ins' and 'outs'; and two party-names were current since the last quarter of the seventeenth century: hence in retrospect the appearances of a two-party system. In reality three broad divisions, based on type and not on party, can be distinguished in the eighteenth-century House of Commons:

[1] *Observations on a late State of the Nation* (1769); and *Thoughts on the Cause of the Present Discontents* (1770).

on the one side were the followers of Court and Administration, the 'placemen', *par excellence* a group of permanent 'ins'; on the opposite side, the independent country gentlemen, of their own choice permanent 'outs'; and in between, occupying as it were the centre of the arena, and focusing upon themselves the attention of the public and of history, stood the political factions contending for power, the forerunners of parliamentary government based on a party-system. Though distinct, these groups were not sharply separated: wide borderlands intervened between them, in which heterogeneous types moved to and fro.

The Court and Administration party was a composite, differentiated body; but common to them all was a basic readiness to support any minister of the king's choice: even in their parliamentary capacity they professed direct political allegiance to the Crown, either on a traditional semi-feudal, or on a timeless civil-service basis, or merely as recipients, in one form or another, of the king's bounty; and adherence to the king's government, so long as compatible with conscience, was far more consonant with the avowed decencies of eighteenth-century politics than 'formed opposition'. A second, concomitant, characteristic of the group was that whether they were great noblemen, or minor ministers of an administrative type, or hard-working officials, or political parasites, they tried through a direct nexus with the Crown to secure permanency of employment: wherein they were, by and large, successful. A third common feature, induced by natural selection and inherent in the character of the group, was that its members did not play for the highest political prizes: peers of the first rank and great wealth and desirous of making a figure in the country, or great orators or statesmen in either House, would well-nigh automatically move into the centre of the arena and take their place among the leaders of political factions.

Here are examples of non-political groups in Court and Administration. The Brudenells were in the second half of the eighteenth century prominent at Court, and although they invariably had two, and mostly three, peerages, and at least four seats in the Commons—'I do not think', says their historian, Miss Joan Wake, 'that they were ever much interested in politics.'[1] The Secretaries of the Admiralty were civil servants with expert technical knowledge, and though from Pepys to Croker they sat in parliament, in the eighteenth century not one went out on a change of government. Croker resigned with Wellington in 1830; 'till our own day', he wrote in 1857, 'the Secretary was not looked upon as a political officer, did not change with ministries, and took no part in political debate'.[2] The Secretaries of the Treasury, forerunners *inter alia* of the modern Parliamentary Whips, were civil servants concerned in the management of the House of Commons. In 1742, the Duke of Bedford took it for granted that Walpole's Secretary of the Treasury, John Scrope, would be dismissed, 'through whose hands such sums of money have passed, and who refused to give any answer to the Secret Committee about those dark transactions....'

... what your Grace mentions is absolutely impracticable [replied Pulteney]. Mr Scrope is the only man I know, that thoroughly understands the business of the Treasury, and is versed in drawing money bills. On this foundation he stands secure, and is as immovable as a rock....[3]

When in May 1765 the king was obliged to take back the Grenvilles, they meant to exact explanations from some Members of Parliament who held quasi-civil service posts and of whose attachment they felt uncertain; but they dropped this design when told by one of them that

he would faithfully support the administration of which he was a part but that he would on no consideration combine with any body of subjects against the undoubted right of the Crown to name its own officers....[4]

[1] Miss Wake, when sending me the eighteenth-century chapters of her forthcoming book, used the sentence quoted above in a covering letter.
[2] *The Croker Papers*, ed. J. L. Jennings, vol. i, p. 81.
[3] The letters are printed in the *Bedford Correspondence*, ed. Lord John Russell, vol. i, pp. 4–8. Their text reproduced above is corrected from the originals at Woburn Abbey. In the letter from Bedford to Pulteney the editor through a slip omitted 'about those dark transactions' followed by fifteen more words.
[4] From Gilbert Elliot's 'Account of the crisis of May–June 1765', Elliot MSS. at Minto House, vol. vii, no. 3; reproduced from a copy in the Liverpool Papers, Add. MS. 38335, ff. 120–33, in N. S. Jucker, *The Jenkinson Papers*, p. 367.

And in 1827 J. C. Herries, M.P., Secretary of the Treasury, thus defined his position:[1]

> I am pursuing my own laborious vocation. . . . I am not in the following of any party. My business is with the public interests and my duty to promote the King's service wherever I am employed.

Horace Walpole admitted that among the 'Treasury Jesuits', as he called them, were 'some of the ablest men in the House of Commons, as Elliot, Dyson, Martin, and Jenkinson'; yet he ascribed to 'secret influence' their continuance in office 'through every Administration', and echoed Burke in calling them 'the Cabinet that governed the Cabinet'.[2]

Whether a post was held by quasi-civil service tenure often depended on its holder. Lord Barrington, M.P., never out of employment between 1746 and 1778, was nineteen years at the War Office under Newcastle, Devonshire, Rockingham, Chatham, Grafton, and North; but Henry Fox as Secretary at War was a front-rank politician. Soame Jenyns, a littérateur of distinction and with good connexions, held the post of a Lord of Trade from 1755 till he left parliament in 1780; for Charles Townshend it was the first step in his political career. The character of Court offices was even more uncertain: Lord Hertford, the head of an eminently political family, who between 1751 and 1766 had been Lord of the Bedchamber, Ambassador to Paris, Lord Lieutenant of Ireland, Lord Steward, and then from 1766 onwards, Lord Chamberlain, wrote to the king on the fall of the North Administration: 'Let me . . . as a personal servant to your Majesty, not be involved with Ministers to whom I have never belonged. . . .'

Not 'to belong to Ministers' was sometimes raised to the level of a principle. Harry, sixth Duke of Bolton, early in the reign of George III sided with the Opposition and rejoined them in 1770; but on succeeding to the dukedom in July 1765, declared that in future

---

[1] J. C. Herries to Sir Wm. Knighton, 27 February 1827, *Letters of King George IV*, ed. A. Aspinall, vol. iii, p. 200.

[2] Horace Walpole, *Memoirs of the Reign of King George III*, vol. ii, p. 221; vol. iv, pp. 75–76.

his attachment shall be to the Crown only—that he sees how contemptible, and weak it is for a peer of England independent as he is, and with a great estate, to be dragged along in the suite of any private man or set of men whatever; and to become the mean instrument of their views, their faction, or ambition.

And Lord Egmont declared in the Cabinet on 1 May 1766: '... that I had no predilection for this or that set of men—that my first duty was to Your Majesty.' Or again, in January 1783, Lord Hood, when put up in his absence as candidate for Westminster, wrote that though he had no ambition for a seat in the House of Commons, he would accept, but would then 'studiously steer clear ... of all suspicion of being a *party man* ... for or against the Minister', as he thought this 'unbecoming a military servant of the King'.[1]

To sum up: so long as government was truly the king's own business, and the king's permanent servants could sit in parliament, there was nothing reprehensible or illogical in members refusing, from legitimate interest or on grounds of conscience, to commit themselves to parties and leaders.

5

The country gentlemen (and certain urban counterparts of theirs)[2] were the very antithesis of the Court party. Their watchword was independence: attachment to the Crown but no obligations to ministers. They entered the House with a sense of duty to the public; their ambition was primacy in their own 'country' attested by being chosen parliamentary representatives for their county or some respectable boroughs (or else they sat for complete pocket boroughs of their own, preferably without voters for whom favours might have to be obtained from

---

[1] *Correspondence of King George III*, ed. Sir John Fortescue, vol. i, p. 27, no. 21, Lord Hertford to the King, 3 April 1782 (misdated by the editor as 1762); vol. i, p. 158, no. 134, Egmont to the King, 12 July 1765; vol. i, p. 300, no. 304, same to same, 2 May 1766; vol. vi, p. 209, no. 4062, Lord Hood, 16 January 1783.

[2] Men like John Barnard or William Beckford—rich business men not seeking government contracts but representative of the independent business community.

Administration). Office, honours, or profits might have impaired rather than raised their standing;[1] the sovereign had therefore little occasion to disappoint them, or the minister to reward them; and they were treated with the respect due to the independent part they played. They were critical of financial extravagance on Court, sinecures, or on costly (and unnecessary) wars; and they were suspicious, or even contemptuous, of the ways of courtiers and politicians; they loathed government contractors and pensioners in the House—the locusts that devoured the land-tax—and were easily roused against them. But not playing for office, they were not bound to factions: when on 12 February 1741, the Opposition Whigs moved for Walpole's dismissal, 25 country gentlemen normally in opposition to him voted against the motion, while 44 left the House.[2]

Governor Pitt wrote to his son on 16 January 1705:[3]

> If you are in Parliament, show yourself on all occasions a good Englishman, and a faithful servant to your country ... Avoid faction, and never enter the House pre-possessed; but attend diligently to the debate, and vote according to your conscience and not for any sinister end whatever. I had rather see any child of mine want than have him get his bread by voting in the House of Commons.

About 1745 the story was told[4] that a peerage had been offered

[1] With regard to honours the position had changed by the beginning of the 19th century: numerous peerages had been conferred by Pitt on leading county families, and seem to have stimulated further applications. On 5 November 1814, Lord Liverpool, having repeatedly discussed the creation of peerages with the Prince Regent, wrote to E. Wilbraham Bootle, M.P., that in order to keep the number within reasonable bounds, it was found necessary 'explicitly to refuse the application of every country gentleman, whatever his fortune or pretensions', and confine new peerages 'either to persons who had claims on the ground of some public service, official or in the field', or 'who were already Scotch or Irish peers'. (Add. MS. 38260, f. 96.)

[2] Rev. H. Etough to Rev. Dr. Burch, n.d., Coxe, *Memoirs of Sir Robert Walpole*, vol. iii, pp. 562–3.

[3] H.M.C. *Fortescue MMS.*, vol. i, p. 18.

[4] H.M.C. *Hastings MSS.*, vol. iii, p. 49; Lord Hastings to his father, Lord Huntingdon, n.d.: 'This I had from Sir Walter Bagott's son, who had it from his father.'

to Sir Watkin Williams Wynn (M.P. for County Denbigh from 1722 till his death in 1749):

... his answer was that as long as His Majesty's Ministers acted for the good of their country, he was willing to consent to anything; he thanked His Majesty for the Earldom he had sent him, but that he was very well content with the honours he had and was resolved to live and die Sir Watkin.

And the boast of the typical country gentleman was that he was neither the minion of Administration nor the tool of faction. Originally the country gentlemen tried to exclude all office-holders from the House; their failure left the door open for parliamentary government. But as a rule they practised what they had preached—it would have been a handicap for a knight of the shire, relying on the support of the country gentlemen, to hold office or to have received personal favours from government: in 1830 Sir Thomas Gooch, M.P. for Suffolk 1806–30, had to make excuses on the hustings for having solicited a Crown living for his son.[1] Before about 1830 even 'too marked a party line' was apt to be considered incompatible with true independence: in 1806, W. R. Cartwright (M.P. for Northamptonshire 1797–1830) was criticized for having consistently supported Pitt when 'a Knight of the Shire should vote as an individual and not as a party man'.[2] In a speech in parliament, on 21 January 1819, Sir George Sinclair, M.P. for Caithness, thus defined the attitude of the country gentlemen:[3]

... neither to withhold entirely their confidence from Government, nor implicitly to sanction their proceedings; sometimes to oppose their measures, but never to impeach their motives—to combine political candour with constitutional vigilance—rather predisposed to approve than predetermined to condemn; resolved to favour but not to flatter; to controul, but not to embarrass.

And he rightly added:

[1] *Suffolk Chronicle*, 14 August 1830.
[2] See E. G. Forrester, *Northamptonshire County Elections and Electioneering, 1695–1832*, p. 92.
[3] *Parliamentary Debates*, vol. xxxix, cols. 55–59.

I am well aware that no individual is more obnoxious to both parties than one who will not absolutely bind himself to either.

Thus the country gentlemen had this in common with the Court group that they too, though for widely different reasons, refused to be tied to parliamentary parties and leaders; further, that they also were neither orators nor leaders: for again, any one of them who rose to such pre-eminence, automatically joined the politicians in the central arena.

6

Little needs to be said about the outstanding, historical figures among the politicians: these were the men who played for the highest prizes, for Cabinet posts and the conduct of the king's business in administration and parliament. It was in their power to procure ease to the king's affairs in parliament, or to obstruct them; they could therefore claim the king's favour, and in a crisis compel it. But who were the rank and file of the political factions? In the first place the relatives, friends, and dependants of great peers usually returned for seats at their disposal; and next, the political following of Commoners who could aspire to the highest offices and hunt as equals with the oligarchical groups. But these followers, in search of places or profits, did not differ essentially from the minor ministers or political parasites of the Court party. In fact, the same men are found at various times on either side of the fence, and happiest when there was no fence: when their group was so firmly established in office that it could hardly be distinguished from the Court party.

Though there were three main groups in the eighteenth-century House of Commons, in action there could be but two: the ayes and the noes, the Government party and the Opposition—which fact has reinforced the delusion of a two-party system. The Government side was invariably a junction of the Court party with a group of politicians; to the attractive force of Crown patronage was added the political ability of parliamentary leaders. When the dissolution of the first Rockingham Administration seemed imminent in January 1766, members forming the core of the official group, in a survey of the political scene, thus described their own position:[1]

> Those who have always hitherto acted upon the sole principle of attachment to the Crown. This is probably the most numerous body and would on trial be found sufficient to carry on the publick business themselves if there was any person to accept of a Ministerial office at the head of them, and this is all they want.

In other words, the Court could supply numbers and workers but not political leaders and a parliamentary façade—for this in 1766 it had to turn to the Rockinghams, or the Grenvilles and Bedfords, or to Chatham. Even when the leading minister was the king's choice—Bute in 1762, Chatham in 1766, North in 1770, or Pitt in December 1783—the king had often to accept some ministers displeasing to himself. But when his relations with the dominant political group were distant or uncertain, he would try to introduce into the Cabinet some ministers of his own: thus Northington and Egmont entered the Grenville and the first Rockingham Administration, and Thurlow those of Rockingham and Shelburne in 1782–3; and it gave rise to comment in March 1783 when the king was not allowed a single member of his own choice in the Coalition Government.[2] The theory of the Cabinet as a joint board of king's men and politicians was, unconsciously, formulated by Horace Walpole when the Duke of Richmond, in discussing Cabinet reconstruction in 1767, objected to Camden because he 'would be the King's'—'I asked', writes Walpole, 'if they expected that every man should depend on King Rockingham, and nobody on King George.'[3]

When a First Minister was known to enjoy the favour of the king, the Court party would naturally adhere to him; and every group of politicians in power tried to fill places at Court, administrative posts, and seats in government boroughs with their own men; these, if their group long continued in office, would

---

[1] N. S. Jucker, *The Jenkinson Papers*, pp. 405–6.
[2] Horace Walpole, *Last Journals*, vol. ii, p. 500.
[3] Horace Walpole, *Memoirs of the Reign of King George III*, vol. iii, p. 47.

permeate the Court party and coalesce with it. But if then a separation supervened, it remained to be seen how much government property the politicians would get away with—places for life, reversions, parliamentary seats, etc.—and how many friends, glued to the flesh pots, they would have to part with. Moreover, men who had long 'upheld the rights of the Crown', condemning 'formed opposition' as factious and disrespectful to the king, found it difficult to enter it themselves: as was seen in the case of Newcastle in 1762, and of Wellington in 1830.[1]

In normal circumstances the king's authority and support were sufficient to keep the average group of politicians in office, but no government could survive for long if either the king or public opinion turned definitely against them. Between 1742 and 1832 the country gentlemen and their city counterparts increasingly became the spokesmen and indicator of public opinion; and that group, about a hundred strong, when solid would carry with it a good many men of its own type and class but of less pronounced independence and normally voting with the Court or with political groups. When in 1764, over General Warrants, a great many of the country gentlemen voted with the Opposition, the Government was in serious danger.[2] When in February 1781, 59 out of 80 English knights of the shire, were listed by John Robinson, Secretary of the Treasury, as opposition,[3] the end was near; and when on 18 March 1782, Thomas Grosvenor informed North 'in his own name, and in those of some other country gentlemen' that they would withdraw their support from his Government, its fate was sealed. Even members of the Court party were now breaking away, or at least absenting themselves from the House: some from conviction, others from caution. When Wellington was defeated on 15 November 1830, only 15 out of 82 English county members voted for him and 49 against; and in 1831 'only six...

[1] See *Three Early Nineteenth Century Diaries*, ed. by A. Aspinall, Introduction p. xxxv: 'Wellington said that he could not bear the idea of being in opposition: he did not know how to set about it.'

[2] See my book, *England in the Age of the American Revolution*, p. 232.

[3] Abergavenny Papers.

English county-members in the new House were anti-Reformers'.[1]

Unengaged in struggles for office, the independent country gentlemen were a retarding element in the growth of parliamentary government, but the charge of favouring 'prerogative', sometimes levelled against them, was as uncorrelated to political realities as were their own attempts at constructive action—for instance in the confusion after the fall of North, when the weight of the independent members was felt more than under stable conditions. Thus early in 1784, 78 members—the St. Albans Tavern group—endeavoured to contrive a reconciliation between Pitt and Fox and a coalition which was probably desired by neither, and least of all by the king: for these country gentlemen party wrangles were meaningless, and a nuisance if likely to bring on the dissolution of a parliament which had run only half its course. Another, even more naive, move in 1788 is set forth in a circular[2] endorsed by 30 Lords and Commoners. In this 'such Members of the two Houses as hold themselves independent of, and unconnected with, the parties that now exist, and are desirous of contributing their best endeavours to promote the general interests of the Country', were invited, while not considering themselves 'under any restraint, or tied down to follow the sentiments of the majority', to 'act in unison with each other. And here is the 'Analysis of the House of Commons' given in the circular:

1. Party of the Crown   185
   This party includes all those who would probably support his Majesty's Government under any Minister, not peculiarly unpopular.

2. The Party attached to Mr. Pitt   .   .   . 52
   Of this party were there a new Parliament, and Mr. P. no longer Minster, not above twenty would be returned.

[1] See *Three Early Nineteenth Century Diaries*, Introduction, pp. xxii–xxiii and xxxvi.
[2] The circular headed 'Proposals' is in the Braybrooke Papers, in the Essex Record Office, Chelmsford (D/DBy C9/44).

3. Detached Parties supporting the present Administration viz:

1. Mr. Dundas 10
2. Marquis of Lansdowne . . . 9
3. Earl of Lonsdale 9
4. East Indians 15

4. The independent or unconnected Members of the House . . . . . . [108]¹

Of this body of men about forty have united together, in conjunction with some members of the House of Peers in order to form a third party for the purpose of preventing the Crown from being too much in the power of either of the two other parties who are contending for the government of the country, and who (were it really necessary) might with the assistance of the Crown, undertake to make up an administration to the exclusion both of Mr. Pitt and Mr. Fox, and of their adherents.

5. The Opposition to the present Administration

1. The Party attached to Mr. Fox . . 138
2. Remnants of Lord North's Party . . 17

6. Absentees and Neutrals 14

The names of Whig and Tory do not appear in this list, nor in any other compiled in those years; nor have I used them so far in this lecture, for they explain little, but require a good deal of explaining.

7

Whig and Tory were 'denominations'—names and creeds— which covered enduring types moulded by deeply ingrained differences in temperament and outlook. But when was a clear party division covered by them? Even before 1714 some scholars now discern merely a number of groups and connexions of a Tory or a Whig hue, or of uncertain colouring; for hardly ever was there anything like straight party voting. About the middle of the century the names were deprecated, described as out-

¹ The number is not given here, but lower down in a summary list of the parties.

worn and meaningless, and yet they were used; for names there must be in a political dichotomy, even if their meaning is uncertain and their use misleading. In parliament even under the first two Georges disaffected Whigs supplied the most inveterate leaders of the Opposition and most of its voting strength. But in a good many constituencies the names of Whig and Tory still corresponded to real divisions: partly perhaps because local factions could hardly have been denoted as 'Government' and 'Opposition', and partly because the most enduring distinction between Tory and Whig—High Church *versus* Low Church and Dissent—retained more vitality and significance in local struggles than at Westminster.

A ruling group will always try to place its opponents under a ban, and the natural consequence of the practice of Walpole and the Pelhams was that anyone who wished to play at politics and for office, adopted the name of Whig: the Finches, Seymours, Legges, Leveson-Gowers, Wyndhams, Foxes, etc. In fact by 1750 everyone at Court, in office, and in the centre arena was a Whig, while the name of Tories, by a process of natural selection, was left to the residuum who did not enter politics in pursuit of office, honours, or profits, that is, to the country gentlemen and to the forerunners of urban radicals.

The nomenclature, as further developed in the first decade of George III's reign, is correctly stated by Horace Walpole in a passage of his *Memoirs*, penned late in 1768, or more probably in 1769:[1] 'The body of the Opposition', he says, 'still called itself Whig, an appellation rather dropped than disclaimed by the Court'; 'the real Tories still adhered to their old distinctions ... and fluctuated according as they esteemed particular chiefs not of their connexion...'; but 'their whole conduct was comprised in silent votes...'. Thus Walpole knew the difference between 'real Tories' and the Court Whigs who had become the 'Tories' of Opposition Whig pamphleteers; but as he habitually flavours accurate perceptions with current cant, a footnote, added in the 1780's, emphatically asserts that Lord North 'was a Tory'. About the same time Burke, in a letter of 24

[1] Horace Walpole, *Memoirs of the Reign of King George III*, vol. ii, p. 67.

D

December 1782, describes the phalanx of 130–50 placemen and place-hunters ranged behind North to secure the survival of places, refers to them as 'the body, which for want of another name, I call Lord North's'; and then adds: 'I ought to have excepted out of the profligates of Lord North's corps five or six Tories who act on principle, such as it is.'[1] Less than two months later, the Rockinghams formed a coalition with the 'profligates' by conceding to them that nothing more should be done 'about the reduction of the influence of the Crown' by economical reform.

Who were now the 'Tories'? The younger Pitt never used the name and after his death his successors went merely by that of 'Mr. Pitt's friends' (apparently George Canning was the only one who occasionally called himself a 'Tory'). On 5 October 1809, Perceval wrote to Lord Melville:[2]

> Our Party's strength, dismembered as we are by Canning's and Castlereagh's separation from us...has lost its principle of cohesion. We are no longer the sole representatives of Mr. Pitt. The magic of that name is in a great degree dissolved, and the principle on which we must most rely to keep us together, and give us the assistance of floating strength, is the public sentiment of loyalty and attachment to the King. Among the independent part of the House, the country gentlemen, the representatives of popular boroughs, we shall find our saving strength or our destruction.

In short: here is once more the basic structure of eighteenth-century parliamentary politics, with increased regard for the country gentlemen but no trace of a two-party system, or at all of party in the modern sense; and the group which in 1760 went by the name of Tories, a generation later is referred to simply as 'independent country gentlemen', the name of Tory being practically in abeyance. It is the history of those party-names, and how they were applied, which calls for careful study free of confusion between names and realities, or rather between the differing realities which the same names were

[1] See E. B. de Fonblanque, *Political and Military Episodes...from the life and correspondence of...John Burgoyne* (1876), pp. 418–21.
[2] Perceval MSS.

made to cover; and next the history must be traced of party realities as shaped by interaction between the constituencies and the House of Commons. Nineteenth-century parliamentary historians now seem agreed in deferring the full emergence of the modern party till after the Second Reform Bill: what preceded it were intermediary forms which should not be treated anachronistically in terms of a later age.

With regard to the second half of the eighteenth century, the idea of party conducive to parliamentary government is usually linked up with the Whigs; which, for what it is worth, is a matter of nomenclature rather than of ideology: the politicians, and not the Court group or the independent country gentlemen, were the party-forming element, and the politicians called themselves Whigs. But among the politicians the attitude to sovereign and party did not depend on the degree of their Whiggery: those who enjoyed the favour of the Crown, and coalesced with the Court party, were naturally less of a party-forming element that those in disfavour, or uncertain of royal support, who had therefore to rely primarily on parliament and seek to form their following into a coherent party. This was specially true of political groups which had forced themselves on the king: the Grenvilles after September 1763, the Rockinghams in 1782, and the Coalition in 1783.

The fourth Duke of Devonshire, the 'prince of the Whigs', was in every way an outstanding personality among them: disinterested and generous, he acted from a sense of duty but according to the canons of the time. As Lord Chamberlain he had to deal in August 1761 with a crisis in the King's Bedchamber.

> Lord Huntingdon Groom of the Stole [he writes] came to Lord Ashburnham who was in waiting and told him that he would put on the King's shirt. His Lordship reply'd to be sure if he pleased but then he must take the whole waiting. The other said no, I will only put on the shirt, Lord Ash[burnham] said I give you notice if you do it I shall quit the room. . . .

And so he did. Lord Rockingham and other Lords of the Bedchamber agreed with Ashburnham, 'were much dissatisfy'd, thought it lowering their employments, and that they could not stay'; but when Bute became 'very warm' over the matter Devonshire warned him that if five or six of the most consider-able lords threw up their employment as beneath them, others too would quit, and Bute 'would get nobody to take it that was worth having it'. The late king, said Devonshire,

> had piqued himself on raising the Bedchamber by getting men of the first rank for them to take it, and that [if] it was lower'd they certainly would not remain in, that it was a very cheap way of keeping them steady to support Government.[1]

Indeed, in 1761 the Lords of the Bedchamber included seven-teen peers controlling at least double the number of seats in the House of Commons, and three courtesy lords, all in the House; and Devonshire was giving the right advice on how to put Court offices to the best use in managing parliament. But in that advice, given by a leading Whig at the end of the so-called Whig era, there is nothing which would even distantly fore-shadow parliamentary government based on party.

For that, owing to circumstances, we have to turn much rather to the Grenvilles. Two months after the king had, in August 1763, unsuccessfully tried to get rid of them, a by-election oc-curred in Essex, and on 28 October, John Luther, one of the candidates called on Lord Sandwich, and expressed his concern at hearing that Sandwich was taking a part against him.

> I told him[wrote Sandwich to Rigby] that I considered myself meerly with regard to Essex as a party man, that my interest and that of my best friends was at stake, as far as related to the support or downfall of the present Administration ... that I had seen Mr. Conyers, who had told me that he embarked himself in my system, and that he meant if he succeeded, to be a true and steady friend to *this* Administration. Mr. Luther answered me that he had given the same assurances to Mr. Grenville ... that he was a friend to *Government*, ... I said that *Government* was a loose word ... was he a friend to *this* Administration, and more so to *this* than he should be to any Administration of which Mr. Pitt was a member, at that he smiled and hesitated a little, but

---

[1] Devonshire MSS. 260. 339.

soon answered that he was a friend to this Administration and would shew himself as such while they acted *consistently*. . . . I answered . . . that his own words obliged me situated as I am to act against him; that this country must be governed by combinations of people, and that those who would act in the combination that I belonged to would have a right to my support. . . .

But Luther, according to Sandwich, kept a back door open by constituting himself 'the judge of what was *consistency* in the Administration'.[1]

Or again, in 1764 the Grenvilles intervened in East India Company elections (the first government to do so), with the purpose of helping Clive to get back his *jagir*, he having pledged himself to support them in or out of office—to which promise he adhered. And when they and the Bedfords were turned out by the king, they withdrew their men from Administration and the Court; whereas a year later, the Rockinghams showed so little understanding of party management that they left Chatham whomever he chose to retain. Ideas and a political practice are things of slow growth; parliamentary government, wise as it is as a system, was not born like Pallas Athene.

To sum up: Parliamentary government based on the party-system, is not an ingenious device, the product of creative thought, for which credit is due to one set of men, while another is to be blamed for lack of foresight or virtue in not anticipating it. Its bases are deep down in the political structure of the nation, which was being gradually transformed during the period of so-called mixed government. An electorate thinking in terms of nation-wide parties is its indispensable basis; and it is therefore at least as much in the constituencies as in parliament that the growth of these parties will have to be traced. In the eighteenth century parliament was without that background of enfranchised masses thinking in terms of party; it was to a high degree a closed arena, with its own life and divisions, still dominated by Court and Country on the peri-

[1] Sandwich MSS.

phery, but containing the forerunners of political parties in the centre. To clear up these antecedents must be the contribution of us, eighteenth-century historians, to the essential work on the least explored period of British constitutional history, the nineteenth century, now started by a group of keen, able, and what is important, mostly young, historians.

4

KING GEORGE III:
A STUDY OF PERSONALITY
(Academy of Arts Lecture, 1953)

THERE WERE three large pictures of George III at the exhibition of Royal Portraits arranged by the Academy of Arts in the Spring of 1953. Looking at the first, by Reynolds, painted when the King was 41, I was struck by the immaturity of expression. The second, by Lawrence, painted in 1792 at the age of 54, depicts him in Garter robes; face and posture seem to attempt in a naive, ineffective, and almost engaging manner to live up to a grandeur which the sitter feels incumbent on him. The third, by Stroehling, painted in November 1807, at the age of nearly 70, shows a sad old man, looking dimly at a world in which he has no pleasure, and which he soon will not be able to see or comprehend.

A picture in a different medium of the King and his story presents itself to the student when in the Royal Archives at Windsor he surveys the papers of George III. They stand on the shelves in boxes, each marked on a white label with the year or years which it covers. The eye runs over that array, and crucial dates recall events: 1760, '65 and '67, '74 and '75, '82 and '83, 1789, '93, '96, 1802, 1805—the series breaks off in 1810; and brown-backed volumes follow, unlabelled: they contain the medical reports on a man shut off from time, which means the world and its life.

Fate had made George III ruler when kings were still expected to govern; and his active reign covered half a century during which the American conflict posed the problem of Imperial relations, while at home political practice constantly ran up against the contradiction inherent in the then much belauded 'mixed form of government': personal monarchy served by Ministers whose tenure of office was contested in Parliament. Neither the Imperial nor the constitutional problem could have been solved in the terms in which the overwhelming majority of the politically minded public in this country considered them at the time; but George III has been blamed ever since for not having thought of Dominion status and parliamentary government when constitutional theory and the facts of the situation as yet admitted of neither.

In the catalogue, *Kings and Queens*, on sale at the exhibition, the introduction dealing with the reign of George III gave the traditional view of his reign:

> Conscientious and ambitious, he tried to restore the political influence of the Crown, but his intervention ended with the humiliating American War of Independence.

Conscientious he certainly was, painstakingly, almost painfully, conscientious. But was he ambitious? Did he try to exercise powers which his predecessors had relinquished, or claim an influence which was not universally conceded to him? And was it the assertion of Royal, and not of Parliamentary, authority over America which brought on the conflict and disrupted the First British Empire?

Let us place ourselves in March 1782. Dismal, humiliating failure has turned public opinion, and the House of Commons is resolved to cut losses and abandon the struggle; it is all over; Lord North's government has fallen; and the King is contemplating abdication. He has drafted a message to Parliament (which was never sent); here are its first two paragraphs:

> His Majesty during the twenty-one years he has sate on the throne of Great Britain, has had no object so much at heart as the maintainance of the British Constitution, of which the difficulties he has at times met with from his scrupulous attachment to the rights of Parliament are sufficient proofs.

His Majesty is convinced that the sudden change of sentiments of one branch of the legislature has totally incapacitated him from either conducting the war with effect, or from obtaining any peace but on conditions which would prove destructive to the commerce as well as essential rights of the British nation.[1]

In the first paragraph the King declares his unswerving devotion to the British Constitution, and shows himself conscious of his difficulties in America having arisen through 'his scrupulous attachment to the rights of Parliament'; the second paragraph pointedly refers to the Commons as 'one branch of the legislature', and gives the King's view of the American war: he is defending there the vital interests and essential rights of the British nation.

A year later, in March 1783, when faced by the necessity of accepting a Government formed by the Fox-North coalition, George III once more contemplated abdication; and in a letter (which again was never sent) he wrote to the Prince of Wales:

The situation of the times are such that I must, if I attempt to carry on the business of the nation, give up every political principle on which I have acted, which I should think very unjustifiable, as I have always attempted to act agreable to my duty; and must form a Ministry from among men who know I cannot trust them and therefore who will not accept office without making me a kind of slave; this undoubtedly is a cruel dilemma, and leaves me but one step to take without the destruction of my principles and honour; the resigning my Crown, my dear Son to you, quitting this my native country for ever and returning to the dominions of my forefathers.

Your difficulties will not be the same. You have never been in a situation to form any political system, therefore, are open to addopt what the times may make necessary; and no set of men can ever have offended you or made it impossible for you to employ them.[2]

Alongside this consider the following passage from a letter which George III wrote on 26 December 1783, after having

[1] Fortescue, *Correspondence of King George III*, vol. v, no. 3061.
[2] Windsor MSS.

dismissed the Coalition and while he was trying to rally support for the newly formed Administration of the younger Pitt:

> The times are of the most serious nature, the political struggle
> is not as formerly between two factions for power; but it is no
> less than whether a desperate faction shall not reduce the Sovereign
> to a mere tool in its hands: though I have too much principle
> ever to infringe the rights of others, yet that must ever equaly
> prevent my submitting to the Executive power being in any other
> hands, than where the Constitution has placed it. I therefore must
> call on the assistance of every honest man . . . to support Govern-
> ment on the present most critical occasion.[1]

Note in these two passages the King's honest conviction that he
has always attempted to do his duty; that he has been mindful
not to infringe the rights of others; but that it would be equally
wrong in him to submit 'to the Executive power being in any
other hands, than where the Constitution has placed it.' And
while I do not for a moment suggest that these things could
not have been done in a happier manner, I contend that the
King's statements quoted above are substantially correct.

In the eighteenth century, a proper balance between King,
Lords, and Commons, that is, the monarchical, aristocratic, and
representative elements of the Constitution acting as checks on
each other, was supposed to safeguard the property and privi-
leges, the lives and liberty of the subjects. Single-Chamber
government would have been no less abhorrent to the century
than Royal autocracy. The Executive was the King's as truly as
it is now of the President in the United States; he, too, had to
choose his Ministers: but from among Parliamentary leaders.
And while aspirants to office swore by the 'independency' of
the Crown and disclaimed all wish to force themselves on the
King, if left out they did their level best to embarrass and upset
their successful rivals. The technique of Parliamentary opposition was fully established long before its most essential aim,
which is to force a change of government, was recognized as
legitimate; and because that aim could not be avowed in its
innocent purity, deadly dangers threatening the Constitution,
nay the life of the country, had to be alleged for justification.

[1] Windsor MS. 5709.

Robert Walpole as 'sole Minister' was accused of arrogating to himself the powers of both King and Parliament; the very tame Pelhams, of keeping George II 'in fetters'; Bute, who bore the name of Stuart, of 'raising the standard of Royal prerogative'; and George III of ruling not through the Ministers of his own choice whom he avowed in public, but through a hidden gang of obscure and sinister 'King's friends'. It is obviously impossible here to trace the origin and growth of that story, or to disprove it by establishing the true facts of the transactions to which it has become attached—it was a figment so beautifully elaborated by Burke's fertile imagination that the Rockinghams themselves finished by believing it, and it grew into an obsession with them. In reality the constitutional practice of George III differed little from that of George I and George II. William Wyndham was proscribed by the first two Georges as a dangerous Jacobite, and C. J. Fox by the third as a dangerous Jacobin; while the elder Pitt was long kept out by both George II and George III on personal grounds. But for some the Royal veto and Royal influence in politics lose their sting if exercised in favour of successful monopolists in Whiggery.

I go one step further: in the eighteenth century the King had to intervene in politics and was bound to exercise his political influence, for the party system, which is the basis of Parliamentary government, did not exist.[1] Of the House of Commons itself probably less than half thought and acted in party terms. About one-third of the House consisted of Members who looked to the King for guidance and for permanency of employment: epigoni of earlier Courts or forerunners of the modern Civil Service; and if they thus pursued their own interest, there is no reason to treat them as more corrupt than if they had done so by attaching themselves to a group of politicians. Another one-fifth of the House consisted of independent country gentlemen, ready to support the King's Government so long as this was compatible with their conscience, but averse to tying themselves up with political groups: they did not desire office, honours, or profits, but prided themselves on the disinterested and independent line they were pursuing; and they rightly

[1] For a fuller discussion of this point see above, pp. 21–32.

claimed to be the authentic voice of the nation. In the centre of the arena stood the politicians, their orators and leaders fighting for the highest prizes of Parliamentary life. They alone could supply the façade of governments: the front benches in Parliament. But to achieve stability a Government required the active support of the Crown and the good opinion of the country. On matters about which public opinion felt strongly, its will would prevail; but with the House constituted as it was, with the electoral structure of the unreformed Parliament, and an electorate which neither thought nor voted on party lines, it is idle to assume that modern Parliamentary government was possible.

I pass to the next point: was George III correct in saying that it was 'his scrupulous attachment to the rights of Parliament' which caused him the difficulties in America? Undoubtedly yes. It was not Royal claims that the Americans objected to, but the claims of 'subjects in one part of the King's dominions to be sovereigns over their fellow-subjects in another part of his dominions.'[1] 'The sovereignty of the Crown I understand,' wrote Benjamin Franklin; 'the sovereignty of Britain I do not understand. . . . We have the same King, but not the same legislature.' Had George III aspired to independent Royal Power nothing could have suited him better than to be Sovereign in America, the West Indies, and possibly in Ireland, independent of the British Parliament; and the foremost champions of the rights of Parliament, recalling the way in which the Stuarts had played off Ireland and Scotland against England, would have been the first to protest. But in fact it would be difficult to imagine a King simultaneously exercising in several independent countries executive powers in conjunction with Parliamentary leaders. It will suffice to remember the difficulties and jealousies which Hanover caused although itself politically inert. The two problems which George III is unjustly accused of having mismanaged, those of Imperial and constitutional relations, were interconnected: only after responsible government had arisen did Dominion status within the Commonwealth become possible.

[1] Benjamin Franklin to the Rev. Samuel Cooper of Boston, 8 June 1770.

Lastly, of the measures which brought on the American conflict none was of the King's making: neither George Grenville's Stamp Act, nor the Declaratory Act of the Rockinghams, nor the Townshend Duties. All that can be said against him is that once the struggle had started, he, completely identifying himself with this country, obstinately persevered in it. He wrote on 14 November 1778:

> If Lord North can see with the same degree of enthusiasm I do, the beauty, excellence, and perfection of the British Constitution as by law established, and consider that if any one branch of the Empire is alowed to cast off its dependency, that the others will infalably follow the example ... he ... will resolve with vigour to meet every obstacle ... or the State will be ruined.[1]

And again on 11 June 1779, expecting that the West Indies and Ireland would follow:

> Then this island would be reduced to itself, and soon would be a poor island indeed.[2]

On 7 March 1780:

> I can never suppose this country so far lost to all ideas of self importance as to be willing to grant America independence, if that could ever be universally adopted, I shall despair of this country being ever preserved from a state of inferiority and consequently falling into a very low class among the European States ...[3]

And on 26 September 1780:

> ... giving up the game would be total ruin, a small State may certainly subsist, but a great one mouldering cannot get into an inferior situation but must be annihilated.[4]

When all was over, Lord North wrote to the King on 18 March 1782:

> Your Majesty is well apprized that, in this country, the Prince on the Throne, cannot, with prudence, oppose the deliberate resolution of the House of Commons ... Your Majesty has graciously

---

[1] Fortescue IV, no. 2451. [2] *Ibid.*, no. 2649. [3] Fortescue V, no. 2963.
[4] *Ibid.*, no. 3155.

and steadily supported the servants you approve, as long as they could be supported: Your Majesty has firmly and resolutely maintained what appeared to you essential to the welfare and dignity of this country, as long as this country itself thought proper to maintain it. The Parliament have altered their sentiments, and as their sentiments whether just or erroneous, must ultimately prevail, Your Majesty . . . can lose no honour if you yield at length . . .

Your Majesty's goodness encourages me . . . to submit whether it will not be for Your Majesty's welfare, and even glory, to sacrifice, at this moment, former opinions, displeasures and apprehensions (though never so well-founded) to . . . the public safety.[1]

The King replied:

I could not but be hurt at your letter of last night. Every man must be the sole judge of his feelings, therefore whatever you or any man can say on that subject has no avail with me.[2]

What George III had never learnt was to give in with grace: but this was at the most a defect of character.

2

Lord Waldegrave, who had been Governor to the Prince of Wales 1752–6, wrote in 1758 a character sketch of him so penetrating and just that it deserves quoting almost in full.[3]

The Prince of Wales is entering into his 21st year, and it would be unfair to decide upon his character in the early stages of life, when there is so much time for improvement.

A wise preamble: yet a long and eventful life was to change him very little. Every feature singled out by Waldegrave finds copious illustration in the fifty years that followed (in one case in a superficially inverted form).

His parts, though not excellent, will be found very tolerable, if ever they are properly exercised.

He is strictly honest, but wants that frank and open behaviour which makes honesty appear amiable. . . .

---

[1] Fortescue V, no. 3566. [2] Ibid., no. 3567.
[3] James, 2nd Earl Waldegrave, *Memoirs* (1821), pp. 8–10.

His religion is free from all hypocrisy, but is not of the most charitable sort; he has rather too much attention to the sins of his neighbour.

He has spirit, but not of the active kind; and does not want resolution, but it is mixed with too much obstinacy.

He has great command of his passions, and will seldom do wrong, except when he mistakes wrong for right; but as often as this shall happen, it will be difficult to undeceive him, because he is uncommonly indolent, and has strong prejudices.

His want of application and aversion to business would be far less dangerous, was he eager in the pursuit of pleasure; for the transition from pleasure to business is both shorter and easier than from a state of total inaction.

He has a kind of unhappiness in his temper, which, if it be not conquered before it has taken too deep a root, will be a source of frequent anxiety. Whenever he is displeased, his anger does not break out with heat and violence; but he becomes sullen and silent, and retires to his closet; not to compose his mind by study or contemplation, but merely to indulge the melancholy enjoyment of his own ill humour. Even when the fit is ended, unfavourable symptoms very frequently return, which indicate that on certain occasions his Royal Highness has too correct a memory.

Waldegrave's own endeavour was to give the Prince 'true notions of common things.'[1] But these he never acquired: which is perhaps the deepest cause of his tragedy.

The defect Waldegrave dwells upon most is the Prince's 'uncommon indolence', his 'want of application and aversion to business'. This is borne out by other evidence, best of all by the Prince's own letters to Bute:[2]

July 1st, 1756: I will throw off that indolence which if I don't soon get the better of will be my ruin.
March 25th, 1757: I am conscious of my own indolence... I do here in the most solemn manner declare, that I will throw aside this my greatest enemy...

---

[1] *Ibid.*, p. 64.
[2] See *Letters from George III to Lord Bute* (1939), edited by Romney Sedgwick, from which all such letters are quoted. Mr Sedgwick's edition is a masterpiece of scholarship. To mention but one aspect: from internal evidence he has succeeded in dating some 330 undated letters.

> *September 25th*, 1758: .... that incomprehensible indolence, in-
> attention and heedlessness that reigns within me ...

And he says of his good resolutions: 'as many as I have made
I have regularly broke'; but adds a new one: 'I mean to
attempt to regain the many years I have fruitlessly spent.'

> *December 19th*, 1758: ... through the negligence, if not the
> wickedness of those around me in my earlier days, and since
> perhaps through my own indolence of temper, I have not that
> degree of knowledge and experience in business, one of my age
> might reasonably have acquir'd ...
> *March* 1760: ... my natural indolence ... has been encreas'd by
> a kind of indifference to the world, owing to the number of bad
> characters I daily see ...

By shifting the blame on to others, he tries to relieve the bitter
consciousness of failure: which is one source of that excessive
'attention to the sins of his neighbour' mentioned by Waldegrave. Indeed, George III's letters, both before and after his
accession are full of it: 'the great depravity of the age', 'the
wickedest age that ever was seen', 'a degenerate age', 'probity
and every other virtue absorb'd into vice, and dissipation'; etc.
'An ungrateful, wicked people' and individual statesmen alike
receive castigation (*in absentia*) from this very young Old Testament prophet. Pitt 'is the blackest of hearts', 'the most dis-
honourable of men', and plays 'an infamous and ungrateful
part'; Lord Temple, an 'ungrateful arrogant and self-sufficient
man'; Charles Townshend is 'a man void of every quality',
'the worst man that lives', 'vermin'; Henry Fox, a man of
'bad character', 'void of principles'; Lord Mansfield is 'but
half a man'; the Duke of Bedford's character 'contains nothing
but passion and absurdity'; etc. As for George II, the Prince felt
ashamed of being his grandson. And on 23 April 1760, half a
year before his accession, aged twenty-two he wrote to Bute:
'... as to honesty, I have already lived long enough to know
you are the only man who possesses that quality...'

In Bute he thought he had found the tutelary spirit who
would enable him to live up to his future high vocation. Here
are further excerpts from the Prince's letters to him:

July 1st, 1756: My friend is ... attack'd in the most cruel and horrid manner ... because he is my friend ... and because he is a friend to the bless'd liberties of his country and not to arbitary notions ...

By ... your friendship ... I have reap'd great advantage, but not the improvement I should if I had follow'd your advice ... I will exactly follow your advice, without which I shall inevitably sink.

March 25th, 1757: I am resolved ... to act the man in everything, to repeat whatever I am to say with spirit and not blushing and afraid as I have hitherto ... my conduct shall convince you that I am mortified at what I have done and that I despise myself ... I hope this will persuade you not to leave me when all is at stake, when nobody but you can stear me through this difficult, though glorious path.

In June 1757 Leicester House were alarmed by rumours of an alliance between the Duke of Newcastle and Henry Fox, and were ascribing fantastic schemes to the Duke of Cumberland. The Prince already saw himself compelled to meet force by force or to 'yield up the Crown',

for I would only accept it with the hopes of restoring my much beloved country to her antient state of liberty; of seeing her ... again famous for being the residence of true piety and virtue, I say if these hopes were lost, I should with an eye of pleasure look on retiring to some uninhabited cavern as this would prevent me from seeing the sufferings of my countrymen, and the total destruction of this Monarchy ...

August 20th, 1758: ... by ... attempting with vigour to restore religion and virtue when I mount the throne this great country will probably regain her antient state of lustre.

Was this a Prince nurtured in 'arbitrary notions', ambitious to make his own will prevail? or a man with a 'mission', striving after naively visionary aims? No doubt, since early childhood it must have been rammed into him, especially when he was being reproved, to what high station he was born; and disparaging comparisons are said to have been drawn between him and his younger brother. He grew up with a painful consciousness of his inadequacy: 'though I act wrong perhaps in

E

most things', he wrote on one occasion. Excessive demands on a child, complete with wholesome exhortations, are fit to reduce it to a state of hebetude from which it is not easy to recover. A great deal of the pattern of George III's behaviour throughout life can be traced back to his up-bringing.

He spent his young years cut off from intercourse with boys of his own age, till he himself ceased to desire it. Bubb Dodington notes in his *Diary* on 15 October 1752, that the Princess Dowager of Wales

> did not observe the Prince to take very particularly to anybody about him, but to his brother Edward, and she was glad of it, for the young people of quality were so ill-educated and so vicious, that they frightened her.

And so they did him for the rest of his life. Isolation by itself would be apt to suggest to a child that there was something wrong with those he had to shun; but this he was probably told in so many words. On 18 December 1753, Dodington records another talk with the Princess:

> I said, it was to be wished he could have more company. She seemed averse to the young people, from the excessive bad education they had, and from the bad examples they gave.

So the boy spent joyless years in a well-regulated nursery, the nearest approach to a concentration camp: lonely but never alone, constantly watched and discussed, never safe from the wisdom and goodness of the grown-ups; never with anyone on terms of equality, exalted yet oppressed by deferential adults. The silent, sullen anger noted by Waldegrave, was natural to one who could not hit back or speak freely his mind, as a child would among children: he could merely retire, and nurture his griefs and grievances—and this again he continued through life. On 3 May 1766, during a political crisis, he wrote to Bute: 'I can neither eat nor sleep, nothing pleases me but musing on my cruel situation.' Nor could he, always with adults, develop self-reliance: at nineteen he dreamt of reforming the nation, but his idea of acting the man was to repeat without blushing or fear what he had to say.

For the pious works which were 'to make this great nation happy' Bute's 'sagacious councils' were therefore indispensable. When in December 1758 Bute expressed doubts whether he should take office in the future reign, the Prince in a panic searched his own conscience:

> Perhaps it is the fear you have I shall not speak firmly enough to my Ministers, or that I shall be stagger'd if they say anything unexpected; as to the former I can with great certainty assure that they, nor no one else shall see a want of steadiness either in my manner of acting or speaking, and as to the latter, I may give fifty sort of puts off, till I have with you thoroughly consider'd what part will be proper to be taken ...

George III adhered to this programme. On his grandfather's death he waited to hear from Bute what 'must be done'. When expecting Pitt at a critical juncture: 'I would wish to know what I had best say. . . .' With regard to measures or appointments: 'I have put that off till I hear my Dear Friend's opinion'; 'If this [is] agreeable to my D. Friend I will order it to day . . .'; 'I desire my D. Friend to consider what I have here wrote, if he is of a contrary opinion, I will with pleasure embrace it'. And when in November 1762 Bute declared he would retire on conclusion of peace:

> I had flattered myself [wrote the King] when peace was once established that my D. Friend would have assisted me in purging out corruption . . .; . . . now . . . the Ministry remains compos'd of the most abandon'd men that ever had those offices; thus instead of reformation the Ministers being vicious this country will grow if possible worse; let me attack the irreligious, the covetous &c. as much as I please, that will be of no effect ... Ministers being of that stamp ...

Two years on the throne had worked little if any change in his ideas and language; nor did the next twenty. The same high claims on himself, and the same incapacity to meet real situations he was faced with: hence his continued dependence on others. By 1765 he saw that Bute could not help him, by the summer of 1766 he had written off Bute altogether. In the spring of 1765 he turned to the Duke of Cumberland, the bugbear of his young years: 'Dear Uncle, the very friendly and warm part you have taken has given me real satisfaction....'[1] And to Pitt, 'the blackest of hearts': 'My friend for so the part you have acted deserves of me....'[2] In July 1765 Cumberland formed for him the Rockingham Administration and presided over it a quasi-Viceroy; but a few months later Cumberland was dead. In July 1766 Chatham formed his Administration; but a few months later his health broke down completely. Still George III clung to him like a molusc (a molusc who never found his rock). 'Under a health so broken,' wrote Chatham, 'as renders at present application of mind totally impossible....'[3] After nearly two years of waiting for his recovery, the King still wrote: 'I think I have a right to insist on your remaining in my service.'[4] Next he clung to the ineffective Grafton who longed to be relieved of office; and when Grafton resigned, the King wrote to him on 27 January 1770:

> My heart is so full at the thought of your retiring from your situation that I think it best not to say more as I know the expressing it would give you pain.[5]

Then came North. Totally unequal to the difficulties of the American crisis, in letter after letter he begged the King to let him resign. Thus in March 1778:

> Lord North cannot conceive what can induce His Majesty, after so many proofs of Lord North's unfitness for his situation to determine at all events to keep him at the head of the Administration, though the almost certain consequences of His Majesty's resolution will be the ruin of his affairs, and though it can not ward off for a month that arrangement which His Majesty seems to apprehend.[6]

But the King would not hear of it. July 2nd, 1779: 'no man has a right to talk of leaving me at this hour....'[7] October 25th, 1780: he expects North 'will show that zeal for which he has been conspicuous from the hour of the Duke of Grafton's desertion.[8]

[1] Fortescue I, no. 74.   [2] *Ibid.*, no. 94.
[3] *Ibid.*, no. 538.   [4] Fortescue II, no. 669.   [5] Grafton MSS.
[6] Fortescue IV, no. 2241.   [7] *Ibid.*, no. 2696.   [8] Fortescue V, no. 3165.

George III's attitude to North conformed to the regular pattern of his behaviour. So did also the way in which after a while he turned against North in bitter disappointment. By the '70s the King spoke disparagingly of Bute and Chatham; and in time his imagination enabled him to remember how on the day of his accession he had given the slip to them both. A month after Grafton had resigned, George III wrote to him: 'I ... see anew that the sincere regard and friendship I have for you is properly placed....'[1] Somewhat later his resignation changed into 'desertion'. When North resigned: 'I ever did and ever shall look on you as a friend as well as a faithful servant....'[2] But incensed at the new situation he soon started attacking North, and treated him niggardly and unfairly over his secret service accounts. George III's attachment was never deep: it was that of a drunken man to railings—mechanical rather than emotional. Egocentric and rigid, stunted in feelings, unable to adjust himself to events, flustered by sudden change, he could meet situations only in a negative manner, clinging to men and measures with disastrous obstinacy. But he himself mistook that defensive apparatus for courage, drive, and vigour, from which it was as far removed as anything could be. Of his own mental processes he sometimes gave discerning though embellished accounts. Thus to Bute in 1762: 'I ... am apt to despise what I am not accustom'd to ...' And on 2 March 1797, to the younger Pitt when criticizing the way measures were weakened in passing through Parliament:

> My nature is quite different I never assent till I am convinced what is proposed is right, and then ... I never allow that to be destroyed by after-thoughts which on all subjects tend to weaken never to strengthen the original proposal.[3]

In short: no after-thoughts, no reconsideration—only desperate, clinging perseverance.

Still it might be said: at least he broke through his indolence. Yes, indeed: from pathologically indolent he turned pathologically industrious—and never again could let off working;

---

[1] March 2nd, 1770, Grafton MSS.   [2] Fortescue V, no. 3593.
[3] Windsor MSS.

but there was little sense of values, no perspective, no detach-
ment. There is a legend about a homunculus whose maker
not knowing what to do with him, bid him count poppy-seed
in a bag. That George III was doing with his own busy self.
His innumerable letters which he copied in his own hand, or
the long documents transcribed by him (he never employed an
amanuensis till his eye-sight began to fail) contain some shrewd
perceptions or remarks, evidence of 'very tolerable parts if . . .
properly exercised'. But most of his letters merely repeat approv-
ingly what some Minister, big or small, has suggested. 'Lord
A. is very right. . .'; 'General B. has acted very properly . . .';
'the minute of Cabinet meets with my fullest concurrence . . .';
'Nothing can more deserve my approbation than'—whatever
it was. But if a basic change is suggested, his obstinacy and
prejudices appear. On 15 March 1778, in a letter to Lord North,
he makes an unusual and startling admission:

> I will only add to put before your eyes my most inmost thoughts,
> that no advantage to this country nor personal danger can ever
> make me address myself for assistance either to Lord Chatham
> or any other branch of the Opposition. . . .[1]

As a rule he would sincerely assert, perhaps with somewhat
excessive ostentation, that first and foremost he considered the
good of the country. When told by Bute that it would be im-
proper for him to marry Lady Sarah Lennox, he replied: 'the
interest of my country ever shall be my first care, my own in-
clinations shall ever submit to it' (and he added: 'I should wish
we could next summer . . . get some account of the various
Princesses in Germany'—and he settled down to 'looking in
the New Berlin Almanack for Princesses'). When considering
withdrawal from the German War, he wrote (with a sidelong
glance at the late King) about the superiority of his love 'to
this my native country over any private interest of my own. . . .'
He was 'a King of a free people'; 'I rely on the hearts of my
subjects, the only true support of the Crown,' he wrote in November 1760. They will not desert him—

[1] Fortescue IV, no. 2221.

if they could be so ungrateful to me who love them beyond anything else in life, I should then I realy believe fall into the deepest melancholy which would soon deprive me of the vexations of this life.

The same note, of love for this country and trust that his subjects would therefore stand by him, continues for almost twenty years. But gradually other overtones begin to mix with it. He had become the target of virulent attacks and unjust suspicions which he deeply resented. Thus to Lord North on 7 March 1780: '. . . however I am treated I must love this country.'[1] And to the Prince of Wales on 14 August 1780:

> The numberless trials and constant torments I meet with in public life, must certainly affect any man, and more poignantly me, as I have no other wish but to fulfill my various duties; the experience of now twenty years has convinced me that however long it may please the Almighty to extend my days, yet I have no reason to expect any diminution of my public anxiety; where am I therefore to turn for comfort, but into the bosom of my own family?[2]

And he appealed to his son, the future George IV, to connect himself only with young men of respectable character, and by his example help 'to restore this country to its former lustre' —the old tune once more. And, in another letter:

> From your childhood I have ever said that I can only try to save my country, but it must be by the co-operation of my children only that I can effect it.[3]

In the 1780s there is a more than usually heavy crop of bitter complaints about the age by one 'righteous overmuch': 'it has been my lot to reign in the most profligate age', 'depravity of such times as we live in', 'knavery and indolence perhaps I might add the timidity of the times. . . .' And then:

> I thank Heaven my morals and course of life have but little resembled those too prevalent in the present age, and certainly of all objects in this life the one I have most at heart, is to form my children that they may be useful examples and worthy of imitation . . .[4]

[1] Fortescue V, no. 2963.   [2] Windsor MSS.
[3] *Ibid.*   [4] Windsor MSS.

With the King's disappointments in country and son another note enters his letters. He warns the Prince—

> in other countries national pride makes the inhabitants wish to paint their Princes in the most favourable light, and consequently be silent on any indiscretion; but here most persons if not concerned in laying ungrounded blame, are ready to trumpet any speck they can find out.[1]

And he writes of the 'unalterable attachment' which his Electoral subjects have shown to their Princes. When George III went mad in 1788, he wanted to go back to Hanover. Deep down there was a good deal of the Hanoverian in him.

His insanity was a form of manic-depression. The first recorded fit in March 1765 was of short duration, though there may have been a slight relapse in May; and a year later he wrote to Bute—

> if I am to continue the life of agitation I have these three years, the next year there will be a Council [of] Regency to assist in that undertaking.

During the next twenty-three years he preserved his normal personality. The attack in 1788 lasted about half a year: the King was over fifty, and age rendered complete recovery more difficult. His self-control weakened and his irritability increased. He was conscious of a growing weakness. Yet there was something about him which more and more endeared him to the people. He was never popular with London society or the London mob; he was much beloved in the provinces—perhaps it was his deeper kindness, his real piety, and sincere wish to do good which evoked those feelings. These appear strikingly, for instance, in his own account of his journey to Portsmouth in 1788,[2] and in Fanny Burney's account of his progress through Wiltshire in 1789.[3] He was not a politician, and certainly not a statesman. But in things which he could judge without passion or preconceived ideas, there appears basic honesty and the will to do the right thing. I shall limit myself to two examples.

[1] *Ibid.*   [2] Windsor MSS.
[3] Fanny Burney, *Diary* (1905), vol. iv, pp. 310–11.

When in 1781 a new Provost was to be appointed at Eton, George III insisted on choosing a man 'whose literary tallents might make the appointment respectable ... for Eton should not be bestowed by favour, but merit'.[1] And when in 1787 a new Lord Lieutenant had to be chosen for Ireland, the King wrote to the younger Pitt about the necessity

> of looking out for the person most likely to conduct himself with temper, judgement, and an avowed resolution to avoid partiality and employ the favours he has to recommend to with the justice due to my service and to the public.... When I have stated this Mr. Pitt must understand that I do not lean to any particular person ... when I state that a Lord Lieutenant should have no predelection but to advance the public good I should be ashamed to act in a contrary manner.[2]

I have given here a picture of George III as seen in his letters, 'warts and all'. What I have never been able to find is the man arrogating power to himself, the ambitious schemer out to dominate, the intriguer dealing in an underhand fashion with his Ministers; in short, any evidence for the stories circulated about him by very clever and eloquent contemporaries. He had a high, indeed an exaggerated, notion of royalty but in terms of mission and duties rather than of power; and trying to live up to this idealized concept, he made unreasonable demands on himself. Setting himself unattainable standards, he could never truly come to grips with reality: which condemned him to remain immature, permanency of inner conflict precluding growth. Aware of his inadequacy, he turned to others and expected them to enable him to realize his visionary program (this appears clearest in his relations with Bute); and he bitterly reproached them in his own mind, and blamed the age in which he lived, for his own inevitable failure. The tension between his notions and reality, and the resulting frustration, account to a high degree for his irritability, his deep-seated resentments, and his suppressed anger—for situations intolerable and disastrous for himself and others; and it may have been a contributory factor in his mental breakdowns. The desire to escape from

---

[1] Fortescue V, no. 3455.   [2] Windsor MSS.

that unbearable conflict repeatedly shows itself in thoughts of abdication which must not be deemed insincere because never acted upon (men of his type cannot renounce their treadmill). He himself did not understand the nature and depth of his tragedy; still less could others. There was therefore room for the growth of an injurious legend which made that heavy-burdened man a much maligned ruler; and which has long been accepted as history.

5

COUNTRY GENTLEMEN IN PARLIAMENT
1750—84
(Enid Muir Lecture, 1954)

In common parlance 'country gentlemen' can be equated with commoners possessed of armorial bearings and landed estates. but the term denotes also a way of life: Colonel John Selwyn was a country gentleman, but no one would describe his son George Augustus Selwyn, the wit, as such—a rustic touch is implied in the term. And there are outer rings to the indisputable core of any social group. At what point do men in the line of succession to a peerage merge back into the country gentry? And what about Irish peers, especially those with nothing Irish to them except their titles? In the mid-eighteenth-century House of Commons, excluding sons of British and Scottish peers on the one flank (an average of about 80) and those with 'no claim to arms' on the other (less than 30) we are left with about 80 per cent of the total. Yet in Parliament the term 'country gentleman' is never made to cover anything like four-fifths of the House; its character is residual: certain categories are subtracted, and not the same by everybody, and what is left is called country gentlemen.

There are elaborate lists in the Newcastle Papers[1] analysing the House of Commons as it emerged from the general election of 1754; and the results appeared of sufficient importance to Lord Hardwicke to copy them out for his own use.[2] A peculiar feature of these lists is that, having abstracted several professional groups—officers in the Army or Navy, placemen, mer-

[1] Add. MS. 33034, ff. 169–181. [2] Add. MS. 35876, f. 1.

chants and planters, and practising lawyers—they describe the
rest as 'country gentlemen', including among them even courtesy lords. Roughly the category is meant to denote men without professional interests and in less obvious dependence on
Administration. And in fact while in the professional groups
only 25 are classed as against the Administration, 6 as 'doubtful', and 170 as 'for' (yielding an over-all majority of 139)
among the country gentlemen the corresponding figures are
124, 28, and 162, leaving a narrow margin of 10.

Still, these 'country gentlemen' on both sides formed groups
of a mixed character. Among the 162 friends of the Administration a great many, while they held no places or pensions, depended on Government support for their seats, and drew
heavily on official patronage for their relatives, friends, and
most of all their constituents; others were connected with peers
or leading politicians in office; and it was a small and shrinking
group of truly independent Whigs of the country gentleman
type which differed basically from holders of places, commis-
sions, or contracts. Similarly on the Opposition side a distinction should be drawn between mere 'outs' panting to get in,
and the real independents; but of the 152 country gentlemen
classed in 1754 as 'against' or 'doubtful', at least two-thirds
were such independents.

The distinguishing mark of the country gentleman was disinterested independence: he should not be bound either to
Administration or to any faction in the House, nor to a magnate
in his constituency; if a knight of the shire, he should owe his
election to the free choice of the gentlemen of the county, and
if a borough Member, he should sit on his own interest: so as
to be free to follow in the House the dictates of his own judgement and conscience. The monumental inscription in the
church of St. Mary, Astbury, for Richard Wilbraham Bootle,
M.P. for Chester 1761–90, reads: 'in Parliament his conduct
was uniform in the support of his King and his country, in the
respectable character of an independent country gentleman.'
And a newspaper about 1780[1] described him as

[1] Some 25 years ago I picked up, I do not remember where, a book of
newspaper cuttings headed 'Parliamentary Characters. From the *Public*

one of the most independent Members in the House. He attaches himself to no party, but is governed in the vote he gives, by the unbiased suggestions of his judgment, and the fair operation of that influence only which originates in the several arguments he hears. . . .

A similar attitude was taken by Lord Belasyse, son of the Earl Fauconberg, but in character and outlook a Yorkshire country gentleman, when he wrote to his father on 20 April 1769:[1]

> Last Saturday I sat twelve hours in the House of Commons without moving, with which I was well satisfied, as it gave me the power from the various arguments on both sides of determining clearly by my vote my opinion. . . .

And about William Drake, Member for his own pocket borough of Agmondesham during half a century, 1746-96, a newspaper wrote in the early 1780s:[2]

> . . . the late Earl Temple took great pains to enlist this gentleman under the banners of the Chatham party; but tho' Mr. Drake uniformly supported the measures of that great statesman, he could never be prevailed upon to form a partial connection which might deprive him of the constitutional freedom of sentiment which *ought* to be the characteristic of a British senator. . . .

Here was a conception of Parliamentary duties radically different from our own: such Members did not deem it a function of Parliament to provide a Government—the Government to them was the King's. Their duty was to support it as long as they honestly could, while judging of questions which came before them with the impartiality and disinterestedness of a jury.

Ledger, 1779; and *The English Chronicle*, 1780 and 1781.' The cuttings are not dated nor marked with the name of the newspaper. At the end there are some cuttings and papers referring to William Strahan, M.P., the printer, and his wife, which suggests that the book may have been started by him, and completed by someone connected with him.

[1] Fauconberg MSS. in the possession of Captain Malcom Wombwell, at Newburgh Priory, Yorks.

[2] G. Eland on 'The Shardeloes Muniments' in *Records of Buckinghamshire*, p. 294. The cutting can be dated approximately from internal evidence.

As late as 1793, R. B. Jenkinson (subsequently second Earl of Liverpool and Prime Minister) in a debate on Parliamentary Reform,[1] described 'the landed interest, or country gentlemen', as seldom ambitious of exercising Government functions.

> Indeed, it may, perhaps, be more proper that such persons should be employed in watching over the conduct of those who exercise the functions of executive Government, than that they should be employed in exercising those functions themselves.

In short, not partisans but judges; and therefore without party label.

Things were as yet somewhat different about 1750 when 'independent country gentlemen' was well-nigh a synonym for Tory. Between 1688 and 1714, Whigs and Tories alike had a Court and a country wing, and neither side being permanently in office, the balance of that double division was maintained. But during the Walpole-Pelham era, the Tories' forty years in the desert, the Court-minded among them, that is most of the nobility and the 'flesh-potters', drifted over to the 'Whigs', while among these the country gentlemen were being gradually absorbed by the Administration group. Thus the Tories were losing their Court, and the Whigs their country wing.

It would indeed have been wholly unnatural, and even priggish, for a supporter of Administration, by a self-denying ordinance to preclude himself from ever asking a service or favour of his friends in office. It was merely a question of how frequent and urgent such requests were, whether the favours were for the Member himself or for others, and what conclusions were drawn from their being granted or refused; most of all, how far the Member would go against his own convictions in his support of Administration. There were country Whigs of an older stamp: such as John Garth (born in 1701), M.P. for Devizes 1740–64, who in 1755 could speak of 'fifteen years' of 'constant and steady concurrence in support of the measures of Government in Parliament without any assistance or return';[2] Robert More (born in 1703). M.P. for Shrewsbury,

---

[1] *Parliament Register* (1793). vol. xxxv, p. 389.
[2] See 'Charles Garth and his Connexions', by L. B. Namier, in *The English Historical Review*, 1939.

who claimed to have been chosen 'without solicitation, without influence of Minister of State or Lord', in 'contempt for the influence of the greatest';[1] John White (born 1699), M.P. for East Retford, and John Page (born 1697), M.P. for Chichester, two strong independent characters. There were also some younger men, such as Brooke Forester (born 1717), M.P. for Much Wenlock, against whose name it was noted in a list of the House prepared for Lord Bute: 'Old Whig', 'by Whiggism attached to Lord Powis as the head of that party in Shropshire, but soliciting very few favours of Government'.[2] And in 1785 his son George, pointing to his own record during 30 years' service as Member for the borough, declared:[3]

> To preserve independence, to support the consequence of Parliament is I conceive the only means of protecting and preserving the rights and liberties of the people, and in order to do that, I will be independent myself whilst in your service.

Most of all, there was the group of Yorkshire Whigs, which hardly finds its counter-part in any other county. There was Cholmley Turner whose 'distinctive characteristic was a dislike of aristocratic domination in the county', and who with the support both of Whig and Tory gentlemen was 'able to show a certain coolness towards some of the greater magnates'. In 1734, and again in 1741, he would not accept nomination from the Whig peers but would await what he called 'the command of the gentlemen' in a county meeting; and 'in 1747, he could not be persuaded to stand again, giving as his reason that there were "so many noblemen" who were "thought to have the interest and direction of the county".'[4] A similar attitude was adopted by his nephew: in 1768 when Rockingham wanted to recommend him as Parliamentary candidate for York, Charles Turner was reluctant to join the Rockingham Club (the society

[1] See *The Structure of Politics at the Accession of George III*, by L. B. Namier, vol. ii, p. 321.
[2] Add. MS. 38,333, f. 93.
[3] Forester MSS. in the possession of Lord Forester at Willey Park, Salop.
[4] See Cedric Collyer: 'The Rockinghams and Yorkshire Politics 1742–1761', *Thoresby Society Proceedings*, vol. xli, part 4 (1954), no. 99.

of York Whigs) since he did not wish to seem to owe his seat
in Parliament to aristocratic patronage.[1] Further, there were
the two Armytages, the three Lascelles, old William Aislabie,
and young Belasyse. And foremost among these Yorkshire
Whigs was George Savile, a close friend of Rockingham's, who
declined nomination by him either at Higham Ferrers or York,
but would only stand for the county, with the support of its
gentlemen;[2] who neither in 1765 nor in 1782 accepted office
from his friends, and during his many years in Parliament
probably never gave a factious vote; and in the list of the Commons drawn up for Shelburne in August 1782, after Rockingham's death, is placed in the residual column of 'country
gentlemen and persons unconnected'.[3]

Still, these independent country gentlemen were a mere trim-
ming to the Whigs in Administration or in Opposition, just as
a few peers were to the Tory country gentlemen. It is the
gradual identification of Tories with the independent country
gentlemen which empties the party name of specific contents.
There were men whom political managers hardly knew how to
label. Thomas Hill, M.P. for Shrewsbury, was nephew and
heir of Sir Richard Hill, a Tory of the reign of William III;
Thomas, who never held any office, entered Parliament under
the wing of Lord Powis, head of the Shropshire Whigs, and
with the support of Sir John Astley,[4] M.P. for Shropshire, an
arch-Tory; and he still appears as a Tory in Newcastle's list
of 1767[5] although he used to receive Newcastle's 'circular
letter', the eighteenth-century Parliamentary whip. There were
knights of the shire such as Robert Shaftoe in Durham or Lord

[1] Rockingham MSS. of Earl Fitzwilliam in the Sheffield Public Library
R1–588 and R78–32.   [2] Collyer, loc. cit.
[3] Dundas Papers in the National Library of Scotland.
[4] Sir John Astley to his agent, 28 February 1748/9: 'Jones, Mr. Hill of
tarn who i mett here i find intends to offer himself a candidate for
Shresbury att the next ellection in cace a vacancy happens you must
imeadetly aply to my tennants that are burggeses or any body i have any
interest in and desire the faviour of them to oblige me with their vote
and interest for Mr. Hill att the next ellection, I am your friend Sir
John Astley.' Attingham MSS. at the Salop R.O.
[5] Add. MS. 33001, ff. 357–363.

Downe in Yorkshire, members of Tory families returned 'on Whig principles' with the support of Administration, without losing that of the Tory gentry. In spite of such uncertainties, it is still possible about 1750 or 1760 to compile a list of so-called Tories; but hardly in 1770: and by the 1780s the designation of Tory is completely replaced in Parliament by that of country gentlemen, 'independent and unconnected'—men not owing suit to any political leader.

There is peculiar difficulty even about 1750 in the study of a nation-wide group without a leader or program or deeper coherence; especially as its members were seldom literary men addicted to writing, and very few collections even of their personal papers have survived. Bolingbroke belongs to the age of the 'pre-exile from office' Tories. Even William Wyndham is still a politician of the Queen Anne period (and his papers seem to have been destroyed). Nor have those of Sir Watkin Williams Wynn so far come to light; they are said to have perished in the fire at Wynnstay in 1858. After his death in 1749, the country gentlemen threw up no leader approximating him in stature. Influential among them, and sometimes acting as their spokesmen, were two men of curiously disparate mentality: Sir John Phillips, the Pembrokeshire squire, long suspected of Jacobitism, and Alderman William Beckford, the richest and most prominent of the West Indian planters, and in the 1760s leader of the Chathamite City radicals. Some papers of John Phillips are at the Welsh National Library at Aberystwyth but nothing of political importance; while those of William Beckford seem lost—the papers of his son, the much biographized author of *Vathek*, survive, but not of the father. In fact, I have so far found only one very rich collection of manuscripts of a Tory country gentleman: that of Sir Roger Newdigate of Arbury, Warwickshire, and Harefield, Middlesex.[1] His experience and the range of his activities were wider than that of most of his fellow country gentlemen. In 1742, he was returned for Middlesex in place of William Pulteney, created Earl of Bath; ousted in 1747, he was returned in 1750 for Oxford University, which he

---

[1] The Newdigate MSS., in the possession of Mr. Humphrey Fitzroy Newdegate, are now deposited at the County Record Office, Warwick.

continued to represent till 1784. He had thus a triple connexion within the group: with the metropolitan Tories, with the country gentlemen of his own region, such as the Mordaunts of Warwickshire or the Bagots of Staffordshire, and with the Tories of Oxford University.

The man from whom Newdigate first heard that he was being considered as candidate for Middlesex, and who in fact proposed him 'as a very proper person', was George Cooke, Member for the county from 1750 till his death in 1768, and in the sixties a well-known Chathamite. In April 1747, when Newdigate's colleague, Sir Hugh Smithson, subsequently 1st Duke of Northumberland, proposed to him to stand as joint candidates at the forthcoming election, Newdigate declined, considering it 'want of due deference to propose ourselves without the authority of a general meeting'.[1] It was etiquette among country gentlemen to await an expression of the sense of the county as declared in such a meeting; and even canvassing would be given a tentative form pending such approval. I adduce one example only, remarkable in that it refers to much less than a county: the borough of Cricklade, converted in 1782 (as punishment for 'most notorious bribery and corruption') into a quasi-rural constituency through the inclusion of five adjoining hundreds. In May 1782, Ambrose Goddard, successful candidate of the country gentlemen against a Herbert of Wilton in the Wiltshire election of 1772, wrote to Lord Shelburne:[2]

> The nature of my situation in the county lays me under the necessity of declining to take any active part in the Cricklade election at least 'till the sense of the gentlemen and freeholders is taken at a publick meeting which is appointed for that purpose the 27th inst. at Wooton Bassett, my conduct must depend upon the result of that meeting.

Information about Newdigate's life, both in the country and in London, can be gathered from his pocket diaries. In a minute

[1] Newdigate's canvass book of 1747, A. 260.
[2] Shelburne MSS. in the possession of the Marquis of Lansdowne at Bowood.

handwriting he entered each day's activities, visits, and interviews, and sometimes even lengthy reports. His social intercourse seems to have been mainly with other Tory country gentlemen; besides calling on each other, they used to meet at certain taverns, the Cocoa Tree, the Horn, the St. Albans, etc.; and in 1755 there are accounts of several meetings convened at the Horn Tavern to settle the line the 'minority', as he calls them, should take over a bitterly contested election petition. These meetings are also recorded, in a derogatory manner, by Walpole in his *Memoirs of the Reign of King George II*.[1]

The Mitchell election, in which Robert Clive and John Stephenson, supported by Thomas Scawen and Lord Sandwich, had been returned against Richard Hussey and Simon Luttrell, backed by the Edgcumbes and Boscawens, turned into a major affair—and for once Lord Hardwicke and the Duke of Newcastle were taking opposite sides. 'The Court members being pretty near equally divided made this election to be of more than ordinary consequence; great sollicitations were us'd to the minority', noted Newdigate on 24 February 1755. Lord Lichfield and George Cooke supported Stephenson,[2] while another Tory, William Northey, favoured Luttrell, and both Stephenson and Luttrell, writes Newdigate, professed themselves 'inclin'd towards them [the minority], but were answer'd in general that they would attend if desir'd but would vote according to the merits'. On the 28th, some 20 Tories, led by John Phillips, voted with Fox, Sandwich's friend and his manager in that affair, who thus carried his point against Newcastle. After this Horace Walpole has a story to tell, unconfirmed by anything either in the Newdigate or in the Newcastle papers: Northey is alleged to have offered Newcastle that, if he would give up the Oxfordshire election[3] and dismiss both Fox and Pitt, the Tories 'would support him without asking a single reward'. Northey, on the same side as Newcastle, may have made approaches to him, but not on behalf of the whole group;

[1] Vol. ii, pp. 12–14.   [2] Add. MS. 35592, f. 162.
[3] Petition against Sir James Dashwood and Lord Wenman, returned for Oxfordshire on the 'Old [the Tory] Interest'.

nor do the terms seem likely. But Newcastle, writes Walpole, would not pay that price for 'nothing but about a hundred of the silentest and most impotent votes' (as if anyone could have controlled the votes of a hundred independent country gentlemen).

> This notable project being evaporated [continues Horace Walpole] the Tories were summoned on the 5th [should be the 4th] of March to the Horn Tavern. Fazakerley informed them that they were to take measures for acting in a body on the Mitchel election: he understood that it was...a contest for power between Newcastle and Fox:...that he for every reason should be for the former. Beckford told him, he did not understand there was any such contest:...were he obliged to name, he would prefer Mr. Fox. The meeting, equally unready at speeches and expedients, broke up in confusion.

And here is Newdigate's account:

> A meeting 63 of the minority at the Horn Tavern to consider what measures to follow in regard to the two contending parties for power. About 40 members agreed as Michael[1] election not advanced far enough to judge of the merits to meet again on Friday.

On that day, 7 March, according to Walpole,

> 62 Tories met again at the Horn, where they agreed to secrecy, though they observed it not; and determined to vote, according to their several engagements, on previous questions, but not on the conclusive question in the Committee.

Similarly in Newdigate's account the meeting resolved

> not to vote in the decisive question in the committee of Michael[1] election but to stay for the report.

On the 12th, the last day in Committee, Sandwich won by 158 votes to 141; the Tories, in accordance with their resolution, having almost all left before the division. But eight remained

---

[1] According to Tonkin's MS. Parochial History, compiled between 1700 and 1730 and now at the Royal Institution of Cornwall, the original name of the borough was 'Myshell, Mitchell or Modishole,... and nowhere St. Michael till of late, to which denomination it has no pretence but vulgar error'.

and were equally divided; their names are given in Admiral Boscawen's report to Newcastle[1]—on the Sandwich-Fox side: Curzon, Barrow, Hanger, and Cooke; against: Sir William Meredith, Sir Armine Wodehouse, Grosvenor, and Sturt. Some twelve years later, Meredith and Barrow were Rockinghams, and Cooke a Chathamite; and in 1773 it was Meredith who moved to abolish in the Universities the subscription to the 39 Articles, a motion of which Newdigate as member for Oxford University was one of the strongest opponents.

Next, on 24 March, Walpole writes:

> The morning of the report, the Tories met again at the Horn, and here took the shameless resolution of cancelling all their engagements, in order to defeat Fox. . . .

And he goes on to inveigh against 'the wretched remnant of the Tories' crowning 'their profligacy with breach of promises'.

> Only twelve of them stood to their engagements; the Duke of Newcastle, assisted by the deserters, ejected Lord Sandwich's members, by 207 to 183; the House, by a most unusual proceeding, and indeed by an absurd power, as the merits are only discussed in the Committee, setting aside what in a Committee they had decided.

But here is Newdigate's account:

> At eleven to the Horn Tavern. 68 met. Sir J. Philips propos'd to disappoint both parties by voting against both and making it a void election. Sir Charles Mordaunt, Mr. Northey, Mr. Crowle, R[oger] N[ewdigate], Mr. Bertie, against it. Nothing in the evidence to warrant it. Mr. Beckford for it. Came away without any joint resolution.

In the House, Phillips

> moved to make it a void election by rejecting the petition too. Oppos'd by Northey, R[oger] N[ewdigate], and Sir Robert Long. Question Ays 201. Nos 178. These questions were carried by the bulk of the minority who were clear from engagements to either side and determin'd only upon the merits which were very strong with the petitioners.

[1] Add. MS. 32853, f. 260.

What, then, emerges from these reports? Some Tories were engaged on either side; a few political leaders such as Phillips, Beckford, and Fazakerley, thought of political manœuvres; but the great body of independent country gentlemen deemed it proper to judge the case on its merits. Their behaviour was highly respectable but politically ineffective.

The next meetings of the country gentlemen recounted by Newdigate deal with the projected inquiries into the loss of Minorca and the reverses in America at the beginning of the Seven Years' War. Here is the entry of 14 January 1757:

> Mr. [George] Townsend's met his brother Charles, Lord Pulteney, Mr. Vaughan, Sir J. Phillips, Cornwall, Sir Ch. Mordaunt, Sir A. Wodehouse, Mr. Bagot, Mr. Fazakerley, Mr. Hanger, Moreton, W. Harvey, Mr. Ward, Ad[miral] Vernon, Affleck, Vyner, Beckford, Northey, Sir R. N.[1]
>
> G. Townsend said he had in the H[ouse] declared he would move an enquiry which made him desire the meeting, that Mr. Pitt and the Administration would support and assist with papers, etc., but desired to be excused appearing at this meeting for fear of offence somewhere but heartily desired an enquiry—consulted what method proper, by secret, select or committee of the whole House? Sir J. Phillips was for the last. Ch. Townsend the only placeman there. P. the questions must be divided—that for America to go as far as the Peace of Aix-la-Chapelle and in a select committee because facts must be reported and printed as in that for the Army. But that Minorca would be best in a Committee of the whole House because it lay in smaller compass. Resolved to leave it to the gentlemen in administration to consider what expedient.

And on 1 February:

> Walked to Mr. Townsend's, met many of the same gentlemen as before. Mr. Townsend said he had a commission from Mr Pitt to say that he would support the enquiry in the House. Desired questions might be settled by the gentlemen. A good deal of conversation and that matter but not the questions were settled.

Thus Pitt is seen sending messages to the Tory country gentlemen though excusing himself from appearing personally 'for

[1] Barring the Townshends, Pulteney, and Vaughan, all were Tories.

fear of offence somewhere'—presumably to George II. The country gentlemen desired to leave the decision 'to the gentlemen in Administration', and Pitt to them. And nothing was settled.

About the transactions concerning the Qualification Bill,[1] January–March 1760, we learn from the Newcastle papers only —Newdigate at that time was serving with the militia. The Duke wrote to Hardwicke on 26 January 1760:[2]

> I saw Mr. Pitt ... who told me Sir John Phillips and Alderman Beckford had been with him from the *country gentlemen*; and tell him they intended to bring in the Bill to oblige every Member to swear to his qualification at the table of the House of Commons ... they wish'd the Administration would not oppose it in consideration of the assistance, which *they* had given to the King's measures. Mr. Pitt said he was for it *in opinion*; and should declare for it.

Thus Phillips and Beckford are seen acting for the country gentlemen; and the measure demanded was in line with the perennial motions against placemen—it might have excluded some hard-working civil servants and humbler politicians, and a few bankrupt parasites, but rich contractors, equally loathed by the country gentlemen, could undoubtedly have produced and maintained their qualification. Attempts further to tighten up the provisions of the Bill were made, arousing opposition. Lord Egmont in the debate on 5 March called it a 'wicked and weak bill' whose principle was wrong and 'leading to an aristocracy'. It certainly had a class character. All that finally reached the Statute Book (33 George II c. 20) was that each Member had to take an oath at the Bar of the House that he possessed the qualification, and to deliver a schedule of his property.

On 2 November 1762, Newcastle, preparing for the battle with Bute and Fox over the Preliminaries of Peace, wrote about a conversation with the Duke of Cumberland at Windsor Lodge:[3]

---

[1] By 9 Anne c. 5, county members had to possess landed property worth £600 p.a., and borough members £300 p.a.
[2] Add. MS. 32901, f. 479.   [3] Add. MS. 32944, ff. 212–3.

The Duke gave me some comfortable accounts of Parliament;
that my Lord Grosvenor and his brother had declared for us; ...
that Sir Walter Blackett and Mr. Noel had declared for us ... that
His Royal Highness had heard that Sir Charles Mordaunt and
several of the Tories would not support this Administration. ...

Legge had similar news about his Tory friends, 'honest sensible
men and by much the best of the corps'. But the Duke of
Devonshire remarked on 30 November[1] that he did not think
'it will come to anything'—wherein he was right.

About the same time, Roger Newdigate wrote:[2]

> I can't answer your Qu. what my party is? I am only sure it is
> neither C[um]b[erlan]d nor Pelham, landed men must love
> peace, men proscribed and abus'd for 50 years together be pre-
> sented with fools caps if they make ladders for tyrant Whigs to
> mount by, I like the King and shall be with his Ministers as long
> as I think an honest man ought and believe it best not to lose the
> country gentleman in the courtier.

Note: 'landed men must love peace'—presumably because of
the Land Tax. Next, expressions of dislike of the Whigs who
had proscribed them so long. But did he desire office? He
thought 'it best not to lose the country gentleman in the
courtier'.

Another Tory meeting, on 24 February 1763, is reported both
in Newdigate's diary and in the Newcastle MSS.[3] Newdigate
writes in his pocket diary:

> Mr. Blackstone and Mr. Ward came to breakfast. Walk'd to
> the Cocoa Tree—a meeting—walk'd to Sir Francis Dashwood's
> Chancellor of the Exchequer to hear the estimates read—Sir
> Charles Mordaunt, Sir J. Phillips and self objected to the mode of
> 50 instead of 40s[4]—to the House ...

[1] Add. MS. 32945, f. 149.
[2] On a scrap of paper which I found slipped into a document of 25 November 1762, Newdigate MS. B.2311.
[3] Add. MS. 32947, ff. 92–3. About that meeting see also *Bedford Correspondence*, vol. iii, pages 210–11, and *Letters from George III to Lord
Bute*, ed. by Romney Sedgwick, p. 191, no. 270.
[4] The figures 50 and 40 refer to the strength of infantry companies.

The paper in the Newcastle MSS. reports that the meeting consisted 'of 60 or 70 persons, Tories and others', and quotes Sir Charles Mordaunt as saying that he

> loved the King; had no suspicion relating to him; but the increase of corps was an increase of expence.

Similarly Newdigate, John Phillips, Eliab Harvey, and Dr. Blackstone opposed the larger army establishment.

In my book *England in the Age of the American Revolution* I compiled a list of 'Tories returned to Parliament at the general election of 1761', 105 for English,[1] and nine for Welsh constituencies. Only four were sons of peers: Thomas Harley, Robert Lee, Thomas Howard, and John Ward. The remaining 110 were country gentlemen. During the next few years disintegration set in among them: a few turned courtiers under Bute, some joined the Rockinghams, another batch joined Chatham in 1766. Of the Tories returned in 1761, 31 died before the end of that Parliament, and only half of the original 114 re-entered Parliament in 1768. Many of their successors were no less independent; but the grievance of their exile-from-office period, imaginary in men who did not desire office, was gone. Henceforth their independence was even more obvious, and even more colourless. There was no longer a group—neither meetings nor spokesmen. For Parliamentary divisions after 1766, I therefore take as test of the vote of the country gentlemen the English knights of the shire, subtracting sons of peers, as mostly connected with Court.

For the crucial division on General Warrants, on 18 February 1764, we have the names of 220 Members who voted in the minority, and of 81 absent; and the number, though not the names, of the majority: 234. As there were two vacancies, the names of 20 members, presumably absent, are still lacking to complete the count. Of the original 114 Tories, 104 were still in Parliament. Of these 41 voted with the Opposition, and 14 are known to have been absent. Of the 20 unplaced Members,

---

[1] pp. 487–90. From that list I would now delete Simeon Stuart, M.P., for Hampshire, and add to it Thomas Noel, M.P. for Rutland: the total remains the same.

at least four have to be added to the absent Tories,[1] which leaves 45 voting with the Administration, a mere majority of four on its side. But three days later, on 21 February, Newdigate notes in his diary: 'Mr. Grenville's levy [levée] where I met most of the country gentlemen by agreement.' There is nothing more about it in the Newdigate papers, nor in those of Grenville, printed or unpublished. Country gentlemen, as a rule, did not attend Ministers' levées. Did perhaps Newdigate merely mean a majority of those he consorted with? So much is certain: that most of those who voted against General Warrants were not in formed opposition to the Grenville Administration, which, bent on peace and economies, gave the country gentlemen reasonably cheap government.

At the next important division, over the Repeal of the Stamp Act, on 21 February 1766, 93 of the original 114 Tories were still in Parliament: 39 voted with the Opposition. We have no lists either of those absent or of the majority; but the total number of absents was 116 which, on a pro rata basis, would yield 20 for the Tories. If so, 34 voted for the Repeal.

For the division of 17 February 1767, on the question of reducing the land tax from four to three shillings, I use the English knights of the shire for my test. The vast majority of the county members voted for the reduction: 52 against 9, while 19 were absent. Of the 9 who voted with the Administration, 5 were sons of peers sitting on an aristocratic interest and not as the choice of the country gentlemen.

Over the expulsion of Wilkes on 3 February 1769, there is an almost equal division among the knights of the shire: 24 voted with the Court, 23 against, while 33 did not vote. But if we abstract the sons of peers, we get 14 voting with the Court and 21 with the Opposition — a 3:2 majority against Administration.

Over the American Revolution, as over the Stamp Act, the feeling of a majority of country gentlemen was probably against the Colonies. Some Members previously inclined to side with the Opposition — for instance Thomas Grosvenor, or even Rocking-

[1] 3 or 4 on a pro rata basis, but men who were politically independent are more likely to have been absent without being mentioned as such in the lists of absents on either side.

hams, such as Lord Belasyse and Edwin Lascelles, henceforth tended to vote with the Government.

From the book of cuttings about Members, 1779–81, I pick out six original Tories who voted with the Administration:

Sir William Codrington (Tewkesbury): 'Has much the appearance of being an independent man. He always gives his vote with the Ministry.'[1]

Assheton Curzon (Clitheroe): '...a man of Tory principles, votes with Ministry, but sometimes affects to be conscientious, by quitting the House when the Minister's question is not agreeable to him.'

William Drake, snr. (Agmondesham): 'A respectable independent gentleman, a Tory in principle, and a great admirer of Lord North, votes with the Ministry in general, but sometimes in the Minority.'[2]

Thomas Grosvenor (Chester): '...a staunch Tory, and votes constantly with Government, and procures places for his constituents.'

Sir Roger Newdigate (Oxford University): 'A rank Tory, with an affectation of honesty and independence.'

Clement Tudway (Wells): 'Appears an independent man, although he votes constantly with the Ministry.'

The writer's sympathies are clearly with the Opposition; yet he does not question the honesty of any one of these Tory Members as he does in many other cases.

And here are five other original Tories:

Richard Wilbraham Bootle (Chester): 'A very honest man, and votes on both sides, according to his opinion, but oftener with Opposition than with the Ministry.'

Richard Milles (Canterbury): 'A man of fair, respectable character. He generally votes with Opposition.'

Thomas Noel (Rutlandshire): 'A very old Member of Parliament, and attends but very seldom. He is an independent man, and inclined to the Minority.'

John Parker (Devonshire): 'Usually known by the name of

---

[1] This statement is not borne out by extant division lists.

[2] Another newspaper describes him as uniformly supporting the measures of Chatham; see above, page 61.

Devonshire Parker, a very honest, sensible, independent, man, and votes in Opposition.'

Humphrey Sturt (Dorsetshire): 'With many peculiarities, is a man of inviolable integrity and a good heart. He supports his character as one of the country members, with great independency and respect, and votes with Opposition.'

In the two most significant divisions of the next two years, the vote of the country gentlemen went heavily against the Government. Dunning's motion of 6 April 1780, 'that the influence of the Crown has increased, is increasing, and ought to be diminished', could not fail to secure their support: although giving old grievances a new turn, it summed up in one striking sentence the country party's inveterate dislike of Government interference in the constituencies, and its objection to placemen and contractors in the House. Of the 80 knights of the shire, 70 voted: 9 with the Court and 61 against. But if we eliminate the sons of peers, the division becomes even more striking: 5 *v.* 55, that is a 11 : 1 against the Court. Similarly when the vote of no confidence in North's government was moved on 15 March 1782, of the country gentlemen representing shires 7 voted with the Government and 51 against: a 7 : 1 majority for the Opposition.

What, then, broadly speaking, was the influence and part of the country gentlemen in Parliament? Their votes being determined by individual convictions, and not by pursuits or manœuvres of party, on ordinary problems they were, as a rule, so much divided as roughly to cancel out each other. But whenever a strong movement of public opinion produced some degree of unity among them, their weight would make itself felt. Faced by the American crisis, they inclined to assert authority and were averse to giving in to rebellion, and their feeling of fairness to themselves told them that the Americans should be made to shoulder part of the burden of taxation. On the other hand, the more far-sighted among them saw that the struggle would be long and expensive and lead nowhere, and these, besides a small group of pro-Americans, were opposed to the war. Saratoga did not convince the anti-Americans; if anything it stiffened their attitude. But Yorktown produced a complete swing over among them, as in public opinion at large, against the American war and the North Administration. The leader of that tiny group of country gentlemen who on 15 March 1782, still voted against the no-confidence motion, Thomas Grosvenor, after the division told North that they could not support him any longer. And this was the end.

During the confusion over the dismissal of the Coalition, at the end of 1783, a body of country gentlemen reconstituted itself in the so-called St. Alban's Tavern group. Their dislike of factious politics combined with the wish to avoid a dissolution and general election. They tried to reconcile Pitt and Fox, and make them unite in a King's Government on a national basis. Lord Sydney, Pitt's Home Secretary, referred to them, in a letter of 17 February 1784, as 'the foolish Committee at the St. Albans'[1]; and Pitt himself wrote that day to the Duke of Rutland: 'The *independents* are indefatigable for coalition, but as ineffectual as ever.'[2] Any experienced political observer could have told them before hand: 'I do not think that it will come to anything.'

---

[1] See *Hist. MSS. Comm.*, Report 14, Appdx. Part I, *Rutland MSS.*, III, 75.

[2] See John Duke of Rutland, *Correspondence between Mr Pitt and Charles Duke of Rutland* (1890), p. 7.

6

THE LONG PARLIAMENT

Mr. Brunton and Mr. Pennington, in their study of the composition of the Long Parliament,[1] have set out to examine what differences in origin, social standing, education or profession can be traced between the Royalists and those who took the side of Parliament; and between the 'original members' of the Long Parliament, that is, those elected before August 1642, the 'Recruiters', elected in or after 1645 to replace 'disabled' Royalists, and members of the 'Rump'. And this is their conclusion:

> We found that the Royalist and Parliamentarian, so far as can be judged from the members of the Long Parliament, were very much the same; and the greater and lesser gentry were not on different sides; that it made no difference whether a member belonged to an 'old' or to a 'new' family; that merchants and lawyers were to be found on both sides... The only significant difference seems to have been that the Royalists were on average ten years younger, and more often belonged to families with a parliamentary history.

On the other hand, regional differences were marked: and class or economic interest was but one, indirect, and by no means the most important, factor in determining the intellectual 'climate' of 'country' or group.

In 1641–2 the House consisted of 507 Members; and with those returned at by-elections before the outbreak of the Civil War, there were 552 'original' Members. But there was no

[1] *Members of the Long Parliament*, by D. Brunton and D. H. Pennington (Allen and Unwin, 21s.).

sharp division into two parties at the outset—nine-tenths of the House were then united in opposition to the existing régime. Of 538 Members who can be classified in the light of subsequent events, 236 were Royalists and 302 Parliamentarians. The landed interest was dominant in the House (as it was in 1740, and even in 1840); and it was flanked by the lawyers and the merchants, who were regarded as distinct groups, and (as also a century later) 'were added collectively to Committees concerned with their professional interests'. Yet in education, and usually in origin, the lawyers and the country gentlemen were indistinguishable; and also land and trade were closely connected—landowners would engage in trade and speculation, apprentice a younger son to a City firm, and conclude 'City marriages', while merchants invested in land and founded county families.

There was a slight preponderance of Royalists among the sons of peers in the House of 1640–2—due, no doubt, to their closer connexion with the Court. But the number of baronets and knights, and also of practising lawyers, of whom there were 75 among the 'original' Members, was roughly proportionate to the strength of the two sides in the House. It is more difficult to define, and therefore to count, merchants: 'including some small local men but excluding those who, despite interests in trading companies, had no mercantile establishment of their own', the total amounted to 45–50. Among these ten Londoners were, with one single exception, on the Parliamentary side: a regional group which finds its counterpart in the rest of Middlesex, solidly Parliamentarian, and in Essex, with one Royalist among its eight Members. Among the merchants returned by provincial towns in which they traded, there was a considerable majority, but nowhere a solid body, of anti-Royalists; and a closer examination of their political allegiance 'does not suggest that commercial interests were in themselves enough to bring a Member to the Parliamentary side'.

The regional distribution of the two parties is striking: the East (Essex, Herts., Cambs., Hunts., Suffolk, Norfolk, and Lincs.) and the South-East (Hants., Sussex, Middx., Surrey, Kent, and the Cinque Ports) returned 42 Royalists and 125

Parliamentarians, that is, a three-to-one majority for Parliament; the West (Wales, the four Border counties, and Worcs.) and the North (Yorks., Lancs., and three Northern counties—Durham was as yet unrepresented) returned 80 Royalists and 48 Parliamentarians—a five-to-three majority for the King. In the Midlands there was a substantial majority for Parliament, while in the South-West the two parties were almost equally balanced (of its three biggest county representations Cornwall was predominantly Royalist, Wiltshire Parliamentary, and Devon equally divided). To explain that formation, region by region, will be the task of further, much more detailed, research which the authors of this book had necessarily to eschew. As they rightly remark, the greatest obstacle in the historian's work is 'his inability to penetrate men's minds'; and whatever he can attempt in that direction requires very careful study of documents and correspondence which cannot be undertaken by two scholars on a nation-wide scale. Some groups will probably be found to have earlier foundations; some may be due to an outstanding personality in the district; and religion will probably prove the most important single factor. In religion itself a sociological component is almost invariably present, but it counts for far less in times of intense religious feeling than in periods of comparative indifference. It is the tendency to read history back (beside the 'materialistic conception') which has produced neat and untrue class theories about the Puritan revolution. Snobbery or, to use a milder expression, social considerations, and material interests did not determine men's religious allegiance in that era.

The outstanding difference between the two sides noted by the authors concerns age and parliamentary experience, two inter-connected aspects.

> The median ages of the two parties for the whole country have been worked out at 36 and 47 respectively—a very large difference.

I would call it staggering. It takes a lot to produce a difference in the median for groups of two to three hundred. The median of the entire House of 1640 must have been about 42; of the Parliaments of 1761 and 1818 it was above 43; and of that of

1945, 46, that of the Conservatives and Labour being the same (though not the distribution between age groups). In every region the Royalists were younger men than the Parliamentarians. There were 172 Parliamentarians against 92 Royalists among those born before 1600, *i.e.*, an almost two-to-one majority for Parliament among men above 40; a slight Parliamentary preponderance in the next decade; and 72 Royalists against 37 Parliamentarians among those born in 1610 or after, *i.e.*, nearly a two-to-one Royalist majority among those of 30 or below. Here is a fact which, when explained, may throw new light on the period—had an anti-Puritan reaction set in among the young by the time the Long Parliament was meeting? Were they getting sick of their stern, austere parents? But before drawing any such conclusion it would be necessary to ascertain the politics of the sons of the elderly Puritan Members, and of the fathers of the young Royalists—which might, indeed, prove an arduous task.

The age median of the Recruiters is not given, only their distribution between age groups. They were even younger than the Royalists: a new generation on the Puritan side. Pamphleteers at a later date

> developed the idea that the Recruiters were obscure townsmen or upstart colonels. It is true that the number of officers among them was large ... Including militia regiments roughly a quarter of the Recruiters held or had held the rank of colonel or a higher one ... A few obscure townsmen who had won success in the Army were elected for their local boroughs; a few richer townsmen who could in any case have expected election held office in militia regiments. But the majority of the colonels in Parliament were gentry ... and they included many strong opponents of the Army's political domination.

Similarly the 'huge influx of Independents and irreconcilables' was a fear before the event, and a legend after: 'many prominent and extreme Independents were Recruiters', but 'Independency was only just perceptibly stronger among the new members than among the old'. The last few inches make a man abnormally tall or small; and statistical statements based on mere impressions are apt to generalize from marginal facts. It is a great merit of this book that it establishes true perspective in place of subjective impressions.

While a general survey is given of the entire country, the representation of two regions, the East and the South-West, has been analysed in greater detail. The chapter on 'The Eastern Association' is by Mr. Brunton, who died in a road accident on 16 May 1952; it is replete with interesting information which, however, has not undergone the last pruning that only the author can give to his work: and writers of mass biography, not to tax unduly the absorptive capacity of the reader, should eschew giving detail which is irrelevant or distantly related to their theme. One feature brought out by Mr. Brunton, modifying the general contention of the book (p. 7) that 'the most important qualification was... to belong to the locality', is the extreme electoral mobility of certain families, especially when backed by Court influence. Thus the Hattons, between 1580 and 1680, sat for fifteen constituencies in twelve counties extending from Lancashire to Wiltshire and Kent; the Jermyns sat for eleven constituencies in nine counties extending from Lancashire to Cornwall and Suffolk; while the Gawdys sat on their own interest for seven constituencies in Norfolk and Suffolk: Norfolk itself, Norwich, King's Lynn, and Thetford, Dunwich, Eye, and Sudbury. Such wanderings would hardly have been possible about 1760; it would have meant encroaching on too many firmly established family preserves, and was attempted by one family only of Irish interlopers.

Mr. Pennington's carefully constructed chapter on the South-West, beside illustrating some of the basic theses of the book, contains much valuable material on the family history of that region. There is remarkable continuity in the Parliamentary history of Cornwall, and most of the leading families of the eighteenth century go back, often in the same houses, to Tudor days, or even to the Middle Ages. To name a few: the Godolphins of Godolphin, the Edgcumbes of Mount Edgcumbe, the Eliots of Port Eliot, or the Rashleighs of Menabilly near Fowey (these last were 'a local ship-owning and trading family which transformed themselves by easy stages into a landed one'). Indeed, Cornwall, with its 21 boroughs and long traditions, would be an unequalled field for the Parliamentary historian, had not several of its richest collections of manuscripts suffered destruction. It is only when he tries to reach the sources of Parliamentary history that he realizes how fast his materials are disappearing. Probably not even half remains now of what there was two or three generations ago.

7

THE NORTH-EAST IN THE
EIGHTEENTH CENTURY

FIVE GREAT sources of wealth have gone to build up the
English aristocracy and landed gentry: the earliest was agricul-
ture; next, mines and metal, foremost coal and iron, copper,
lead, and tin; third, in point of time, came urban rents; in
certain periods, fortunes made in the King's service or in the
law; and in all periods, City fortunes and 'City marriages'.[1]
If the History of Parliament based on its personnel, that is, on
a highly representative cross-section of the 'political nation',
succeeds in supplying data for even approximate outlines of
that growth, we shall have written an important chapter of
English social history. But prerequisite to such a survey are
hundreds of well-documented monographs about individuals,
families, or regions.

Professor Hughes's new book, *North Country Life in the
Eighteenth Century*, bearing the sub-title 'The North East,
1700–1750', proves how much can be achieved by a thorough
search for local sources and a patient analysis of the materials
they yield. His work is based primarily on the manuscripts of
a number of Northumbrian and Durham families: Cotesworth
and Ellison, Bowes, Liddell, Ridley, etc.; and it shows what

[1] Some would name 'sugar'—the West Indian plantations—as a sixth
source. I doubt whether it can rank with the others. The West Indians
cut a great figure in London society, but I suppose on closer inquiry it
will be found that the coal mines, say of Northumberland, Co. Durham,
and Yorkshire alone, added greater numbers to Debrett and Burke than
all the treasure islands of the Caribbean.

amazingly rich sources can be tapped by breaking away from the traditional concentration on metropolitan politics and life, and on the activities of leading statesmen. Of the families which appear in Professor Hughes's book, some were already country gentry at the opening of the eighteenth century, others were founded by self-made men; but the spectacular rise of them all was bound up with developments which transformed the social and economic character of the North-East.

The sixteenth century found the Border country 'much in poverty and penury', the seventeenth was a period of disasters: the Scottish military occupation, 1639–41, and sequestrations and confiscations by the victorious Roundheads; Royalists and Roman Catholics being specially numerous in the feudal North. By 1715, there was scarcely a Roman Catholic gentleman in Northumberland whose estates were not heavily mortgaged— 'indeed, one begins to suspect,' writes Hughes, 'that the last civil war in England, the Jacobite Fifteen, was due, in no small degree, to the desperate poverty of the northern Catholic gentry,' and that the rising was the occasion rather than the cause of the elimination of many old families. Their estates were bought by new men who had made their money in trade, or by merchant families, like the Liddells, who had already entered the ranks of the gentry; and in wealth both outstripped by far their predecessors. Owing to the greatly retarded social and political development of the North, the rise of the landed gentry, 'the most notable social phenomenon in the making of Modern England', occurred here a century and a half later than in most of the country, while the Industrial Revolution occurred much earlier: Newcastle is 'the centre of what is in all probability the oldest industrial region' of England. Thus the great age of the gentry in those counties was made possible by the profits derived from trade, mainly coal mining and satellite enterprises: which produced 'a greater fusion of landed and merchant interest in these parts than elsewhere.' Yeomen grew into merchants, and merchants into gentry; and throughout the eighteenth century the new northern gentry, the Liddells, Carrs, Ellisons, Ridleys, and Blacketts, for example, continued to intermarry with local merchant families.

The most important single collection of papers used by Professor Hughes is that of William Cotesworth, a name little known hitherto owing to the early failure of the family in the male line. Described by Hughes as the prototype of the new rising men, Cotesworth was a yeoman's son; born *c.* 1670, in Teesdale, he was apprenticed to a mercer and tallow-chandler of Gateshead; formed a partnership with his late master's son; and for more than twenty years the tallow and candle business constituted his main trading interest: he worked for the London wholesale market, and for local consumption, especially in the coal- and lead-mines. 'Some idea of . . . the candle-trade alone may be gained from Cotesworth's accounts with Sir Henry Liddell for a single year, 1716—£237 17*s*. 1½*d*. for the collieries, £6 10*s*. 7*d*. "for the house".' But by 1705, Cotesworth was engaged in a highly miscellaneous trade, 'exporting grindstones, lead, glass bottles, and later salt to Holland, Hamburg, and the Baltic ports, and importing flax, hemp, madder, and whalebone in return'; and buying indigo, dyestuffs, hops, sugar, and tobacco in the London market: as he put it himself, he traded 'in anything he could gain by'. Next he turned to a form of transport business anticipating railways: in 1705 he

> obtained from the dean and chapter of Durham a lease, jointly with Dean Montague himself, of exclusive way-leave rights for a term of twenty years with leave to build a wagon-way for the carriage of coals and grindstones to Jarrow staith from half a dozen adjoining parishes. He came to specialize in obtaining way-leave rights of this kind, thereby threatening to hold to ransom coal-owners of the neighbouring hinterland.

By 1710 he himself held shares in various collieries; and next started buying up salt-pans: he could use in them small coal unfit for the London market. By 1715 he claimed to be the biggest salt proprietor in the country, paying over £1,000 a year in duties, and holding the contract for supplying the Victualling Office. But even more important became his coal interests. In 1711, he negotiated for his brother-in-law, Alderman Ramsay, the purchase of Gateshead and Whickham, 'once reputed to be the richest coal-bearing manors in the country'; and on

Ramsay's death, in 1716, that estate passed to Cotesworth. Moreover, since 1710 he had been the moving spirit and paid secretary of a powerful coal cartel or 'Regulation'.

The coal-trade is naturally given pride of place in Professor Hughes's book, of which about one-fourth is taken up by the chapter specifically dealing with it. Its story is told in concrete terms: as lived by a representative group of men. First there is the development and technique of coal-mining, and its finance; and next the great problem of marketing the coal. At times it was, in the words of one deeply concerned in it, 'a fighting trade run in a tempestuous shallow stream'. Yet another one wrote:

> There will always be something to fight about in the coal-trade though for all that, there's few that gets into the trade that is willing for to [go?] out, the profit is so great.

And W. B. Bowes, one of the leading Durham coal-owners, wrote in 1720: 'The colliery never made less than £1,500 per annum these last thirty years past, and made me last year £2,500.'

The question of 'way-leaves' was as burning a problem in those early decades of the eighteenth century as that of canals became in its second half: their course often determined what mines could be worked with profit. Next there was the problem of the ports: the great concern of the coal interests on the Tyne was the competition of Sunderland which had virgin seams in its immediate hinterland, had no old privileged bodies to 'oppress' its traders, and was some hours' sailing time nearer the London market. This naturally led to attempts to 'regulate' by agreement the proportions of the rival ports; and the names of those engaged in such negotiations give an idea of the character and standing of the leading men in the trade: Colonel George Liddell (M.P. for Berwick), writing in 1731 to Cotesworth, like himself from the Tyne, mentions as spokesmen of the Wear interests Lord Scarbrough, J. Hedworth (M.P. for Co. Durham, 1713–47) and H. Lambton (M.P. for Durham City, 1733–61). But whatever the differences between the two groups, they were faced by common marketing problems, and had a common battle to fight with the ships' masters, the London lightermen, and the London dealers. Each of these groups, in order to hold its own, had to organize itself—there would have been anarchy and waste if they had not. Yet such 'combinations' were 'in restraint of trade', and savoured of a 'monopoly' calculated to raise the price of coal. This would affect the London consumer, and bring the City and its representatives into the fray. Prosecutions, Parliamentary inquiries, and legislation to prevent such combinations would follow. And each party would have M.P.s among its spokesmen: the coal-owners would be represented by Northumberland and Durham Members (or some of their body sitting for outside constituencies—for instance, the Wortleys); the ship-masters by Members for Scarborough, Yarmouth, etc.; and the consumer by men like Sir John Barnard and Sir William Thompson, Members for the City of London, or perhaps also by some brewers and distillers —great consumers of coal—with seats in the House. In 1729, at a conference at the Guildhall, in which the coal-owners met the Lord Mayor and aldermen, 'seven distinguished representatives of the Tyne owners, including four M.P.s, were present, and Mr. Hedworth and Baron Hilton for Wear owners'. So far insufficient attention has been paid to that aspect of Parliament and of the activities of its Members: there was as yet no 'welfare State', but there was a State which looked after production and had to deal with a multitude of new problems raised by changes in its methods and in transport; and more patient, honest work was done in this matter by Members with local knowledge and local interests, and inspired by the exuberant and creative spirit of the time, than they and their period are credited with.

'Local issues . . .,' writes Professor Hughes, ' —the Wear navigation in 1747 and 1760 [in elections for Durham city], the threat to the time-honoured grazing rights of Newcastle freemen on the Town Moor in 1774—were the staple of politics in the eighteenth century.' Even the subjects on which the Northumberland and Durham Members spoke in the House were mostly local; and they themselves were, as a rule, of the county (least at Berwick, a Government borough 'where a combination of military, ordnance, custom house, and post office tipped the balance'). There was remarkable continuity in the representation of Durham city: a Lambton represented it in unbroken succession from 1733 to 1813, and a Tempest from 1742 to 1800, when the male line became extinct. 'There is no case of a local tradesman being returned for the city during the century . . .'

At Newcastle the picture is rather different. Sir Henry Liddell of Ravensworth was Member from 1700 to 1710 (he still owned a family house in the town); William Wrightson, Member from 1710–1722, had married a local merchant's daughter; while William Carr (1722–34), the Blacketts (1710–77), the Fenwicks (1727–47), and the Ridleys (1747–1836) all had long-established trading connexions in the town . . . It is significant that the attempts of a powerful 'stranger' like George Bowes of Streatlam to insinuate himself into the borough by getting himself made a freeman were frustrated.

But what about 'Whigs' and 'Tories' in a region where in view of the strength of Catholics and Non-Jurors, and the proximity of Scotland, those divisions had been specially marked and could be expected to survive longer? At a by-election in 1748, a 'Tory' country gentleman, R. Algood, stood for Northumberland against Lord Ossulston (eldest son of Lord Tankerville), the official Whig candidate. H. T. Carr wrote about it to Henry Ellison, his brother-in-law (they were married to the two daughters of William Cotesworth):

I should certainly vote for Lord O. if he had been opposed by any person reasonably suspected of Jacobitism, but considering Mr. Algood's good character and his zealous behaviour in the late Rebellion, I cannot bring myself to vote against him in favour of the son of a man who, though Lord Lieutenant of the County, deserted it so shamefully in the time of danger and who himself seems to have nothing said in his favour but that he is a Whig set up by the Whig Party, who I wish had made choice of a man of more merit, as I think we shall look a little too sour and shew ourselves too irreconcilable to the bare name of a Tory if we can't be so far soften'd and reconciled by Mr. Algood's behaviour as to look upon him almost as one of ourselves, but must to a man oppose him.

And Robert Ellison, a kinsman of Henry's and Collector of Customs at Newcastle, reported though apparently he himself favoured Ossulston: 'The general bent of the people's inclination is to Mr. Algood in preference to Lord O.'; and he added that there was personal resentment against Ossulston: 'he being a stranger in the country and military gent and son of a peer are most industriously propagated'—arguments most effective in eighteenth-century county elections though hardly of a 'party' character. And Algood, not Ossulston, was returned with the support even of 'several of the Dissenters, nay some of the Ministers. . . .'

Even more remarkable was the by-election in Co. Durham caused in 1760 by the death of George Bowes. The Whig candidate was Sir Thomas Clavering; Lord Ravensworth, one of his supporters, wrote about him to the Duke of Newcastle: 'His is a very old family in the county, it has been as true a one for the Protestant Succession and to the present Royal Family, I may say, without exception as any in it.' But the Earl of Darlington, another prominent Whig, head of the powerful Vane family, and a relative and political associate of the Duke, had forestalled Ravensworth and secured the Duke's support for Robert Shafto. Newcastle's embarrassment was increased still further by the discovery that Shafto's father and family 'were always very violent Tories', though 'this gentleman I hear is not'. The Duke had felt certain all along that the Tories would 'take the side where they can do the most mischief', and now he foresaw that because of Shafto's family antecedents they would incline toward him. He therefore appealed for help and mediation to Trevor, Bishop of Durham, and as such in control of one of the greatest electoral interests in the county. But Trevor meant first to feel its pulse at the general meeting: he would not risk appearing on the weaker side, and would therefore follow, and not try to force, the bent of the county. He wrote to the Duke of Newcastle on 7 October 1760, the day before the general meeting:

> Shafto has been with me to declare his attachment to the Govt., in which I believe him sincere, but the Tories are certainly pleased with his standing and glad to join him. The run for him is certainly very great and he gets on much faster without expence than the other does with it. . . .

And again on the day after the meeting: 'Mr. Shafto in the meeting declared his attachment to the Govt. upon Whig principles....' And so Shafto had the support of the Tories although he stood 'upon Whig principles', and of the Duke of Newcastle, Lord Darlington, and the Bishop of Durham, in spite of his Tory antecedents. Let those who know everything about Whigs and Tories, and confidently operate with those denominations, disentangle such politics in terms of parties.

A new and remarkable intervention on the side of Clavering was a circular addressed by John Wesley to the Methodists on 20 November 1760:

> I earnestly desire all who love me to assist him—to use the utmost of their power: what they do, let them do it with all their might: Let not sloth nor indolence hurt a good cause; only let them not rail at the other candidates. They may act earnestly and yet civilly. Let all your doings be done in charity and at the peril of your souls receive no bribe.

Shafto won the election, and retained the seat until 1768; Clavering held it from 1768 till 1790. And here I add a few facts concerning these two Members for Co. Durham for the benefit (and exercise) of those who continue to attach the labels of 'W' and 'T' to the names of Members in the reign of George III. Shafto, the 'Tory', voted against General Warrants in 1764, and in 1765 received a Secret Service pension from the Rockingham Administration; Clavering, the 'Whig', in his first years in Parliament seems to have voted with the Opposition, but during the American Revolution, though independent and occasionally voting on the popular side, he supported Lord North and adhered to him till the end in March 1782.

8

THE EAST INDIA COMPANY

THE EAST INDIA COMPANY, or, to give it its full name, the
United Company of Merchants of England trading to the East
Indies, was formed in 1709 through a union of the 'Old' and
the 'New' Companies. From the outset it had to encounter
European rivals supported by their own Governments, and to
carry on commerce sword in hand in an India where the power
of the Moguls was crumbling. This need of armed support increased its dependence on the Crown, from whom it anyhow
held its charter and trading monopolies: thus a close association
with the Government was inevitable, which exposed the Company to difficulties and perils in times of political crisis. Happiest for it were therefore the days of Walpole and Henry Pel-
ham: it was then that it became

> the prosperous, respectable, and sound commercial and financial
> corporation which was not only far and away the biggest and
> most complicated trading organization of the country, but was
> (together with the Bank of England and the South Sea Company)
> the centre of the financial market rising in London and of the
> Government's political and financial interest there.[1]

Its management was in a chairman, deputy chairman, and in
24 directors elected annually by the Court of Proprietors, in
which every holder of at least £500 stock had a vote, and one
vote only, however great his holdings. The membership of the
Court of Directors was remarkably permanent in the reign of

---

[1] Lucy S. Sutherland: *The East India Company in Eighteenth-Century
Politics.*

the first two Georges; the 'House list' submitted by the out-going executive was carried without much difficulty by the prestige of its leaders, and by a voting strength built up on patronage, on merchant shareholders dealing with the Company, the shipping interest, etc. The business organization of the Company was efficient; the produce of its sales about the middle of the century was roughly £2m. a year; its shares were widely held; and a good many of its directors sat in Parliament, without the Company as such engaging in political controversy. But about 1746 conditions began to deteriorate: there were war with France, conflicts with rival Indian rulers, and growing difficulty in controlling the Company's own servants; and 10 or 12 years later, a permanent crisis supervened in its affairs.

> The new period was to see ... English control spread over the neighbouring Indian territories and an expansion of territorial power which [was] ..: inevitable but which, thanks to ... the spectacular exploits of Clive ... came more suddenly than anyone could have expected. The Company had long experience of the problems of government as well as those of the administration of commerce; but now ... those of government ... began to prevail. In addition ... the new period brought ... a desperate struggle in England for the control of the Company's political machine ... between Robert Clive, the Company's greatest soldier, and Laurence Sulivan, its ablest ruler since Sir Josia Child ... a struggle involving issues vital for the Company and the State, but one in which personal hatreds and personal interests played the greatest part.... The period was also to see the re-entry of East Indian affairs into the sphere of party politics and the inter-vention of the State in the affairs of a Company become at once so rich and so disordered. There was Chatham's first intervention in 1766–7, Lord North's Regulating Act ..., Fox's India Bill, Pitt's India Act, and, as a sequel, the long-drawn-out agony of Warren Hastings' impeachment.

It was the story of 'a company struggling to adapt itself to totally new responsibilities oversea, hampered at every turn by disor-ganization arising from too-sudden wealth and the speculation born of it'; and of shifting Governments and violent Oppositions, whose component groups found advantage in forming con-nexions with interests and groups within the distracted Company.

A rich historical literature on East Indian questions during this period has hitherto been focused on a few great figures and their exploits in the field, in administration, or in Parliament. But of the history of the Company itself, its management, negotiations, and internal struggles, and its relations with Government and Parliament, that 'intricate and often unedifying background' to more spectacular activities and scenes, no proper analysis had so far been attempted: hence a fragmentation of that history which rendered it well-nigh impossible to see its disjointed sequence in perspective. And yet Indian affairs impinge all along on British domestic history during the first 25 years of the reign of George III, and deeply affect its course. It was high time that they were elucidated and worked into the pattern of which they are an essential part. This has now been achieved by Miss L. S. Sutherland in her book on *The East India Company in Eighteenth-Century Politics*, a piece of historical research so thorough and comprehensive in its groundwork, and so masterly and lucid in its presentation, that it must rank among the foremost works on the period, a standby and directive for students in cognate fields, and a secure foundation for further research in its own. Miss Sutherland's knowledge of City finance and politics in the eighteenth century, and also the practical experience of administration which she acquired during the last war, have served her well in her study of the East India Company; she has been able fully to appreciate the problems of its day-to-day management, to value the work of a Laurence Sulivan, and to pay well-deserved tribute to the honest and intelligent labours of John Robinson and Charles Jenkinson, forerunners of the modern Civil Service: administrators who laid the foundations for constructive reform in India but, despised by men of fashion in their day and maligned by orators and pamphleteers, continue to appear as sinister or suspect figures in books of a well-known type. Still, while doing justice to these men, and also to Warren Hastings, 'the greatest Company servant of his day', Miss Sutherland takes a lenient, and even generous, view of his persecutor, Burke.

He may have adopted the East Indian question for party and personal reasons; he may have placed his trust in most unworthy witnesses, in his contemptible cousin William . . . and the virulent and disappointed Francis . . . ; and he showed far more interest in exposing abuses and attacking individuals than in working out a constructive policy of reform. But he was sincere in his savage anger, had mastered a mass of complicated information and . . . was undoubtedly one of the formative influences on the development of a government policy for India.

Laurence Sulivan spent more than 20 years in India; owed his advance in the Company's service solely to his competence; returned to England in 1752 a wealthy but not a rich man, and further improved his fortune in the City; was elected a director in 1755, and deputy chairman in 1757, when developments in India called for men with Indian experience; and entered Parliament in 1762. Meantime Clive by his Arcot campaign, the recapture of Calcutta, and the battle of Plassey laid the foundations of British rule in India; but there was a price to pay: his example and victories did a great deal to upset the precarious balance between public and private interest hitherto observed by the Company's servants. Convention allowed senior officials to make fortunes 'through the recognized channels of perquisite, private trade, and money-lending'; but Clive, having replaced Siraj-ud-daula by Mir Jafar, accepted from him more that £200,000 in presents and an annual *jagir* of £27,000: the first of the gainful interventions in conflicts between native rulers. Moreover, as conquerors the Company's servants now freely extended their private trade in the hinterland, making profits and committing abuses; thus enriched they became unmanageable, or if recalled came back acutely hostile to the directors, spreading disorganization to the headquarters in London; lastly, servants of the Company in India would remit their gains to England by bills on it, after having laid out the money on occasions and terms largely of their own making: all this at a time when the administrative responsibilities of the Company were rapidly increasing.

A split among the directors produced a contested election in 1758; Sulivan's side was victorious; he was elected chairman, and retained control for the next six years. In that election he had Clive's support. But a General Letter which Sulivan sent to

Bengal in March 1759, with bitter reproaches for remittances, etc., gave umbrage to Clive, although Sulivan had taken care to dissociate him from the criticism. 'The seeds of the great feud had been thrown.'

Clive returned home in 1760, determined to cut a great figure in the country. The *jagir*, the fee of a purely nominal office under the Mogul, became his dominant concern, overriding every other consideration. 'My future power, my future grandeur,' he wrote to a friend, 'all depend on the receipt of the jaghire money'; and again: 'Believe me there is no other interest in this kingdom but what arises from great possessions'— had he stayed in India and acquired a yet greater fortune, he might have been 'an English Earl with a Blue Ribbon'. But the Company hesitated to recognize his *jagir* by transferring to him a yearly rent for lands near Calcutta payable by the Company to the Nawab, who still owed them reparation for damage suffered from his predecessor. The peace negotiations of 1762–3 increased ill-feeling between Sulivan and Clive—there was no conflict of principle, but Clive, excluded from a share in the intricate discussions, attacked the terms which Sulivan had accepted; and when a formed opposition arose over them in the Company, he announced his adherence to it. 'The great Civil War of the Company had broken out.'

The election of directors in April 1763 was marked by new and ominous features: large-scale organizations were set up for the production of faggot-votes—East India stock was bought and holdings were 'split' to create voting qualifications; the Government, whose Peace Treaty was impugned, intervened in favour of Sulivan (Fox using the resources of the Pay Office); consequently the Parliamentary Opposition aided Clive; and both sides rounded up supporters. Sulivan won; and payment of Clive's *jagir* was stopped by order from India House. He appealed for help to the Opposition, but was told that it was hopeless to raise the matter in Parliament. To save his *jagir* he now swore fealty to the Grenville Administration; still, the compromise which they tried to patch up for him was rejected by the directors. But his chance came when news reached

London of administration chaos and renewed fighting in Bengal; his return to India was urged by anxious stockholders; he, however, refused while Sulivan headed the Direction; and at the ensuing, bitterly contested, election in April 1764, Clive had the support of the Government. The result was a dead-heat; but soon Sulivan's following began to crumble; Clive's demand for recognition of his *jagir* for 10 years was accepted; and he sailed for Bengal, armed with wide discretionary power. The election of 1765 completed his victory over Sulivan—he had won a decisive round. Still, as early as May 1764, Charles Jenkinson wrote:

> The affairs of this Company seem to be become much too big for the management of a body of merchants ... these disputes will probably end in a Parliamentary enquiry.

In April 1766 news reached London of Clive having assumed, on behalf of the Company, control of Bengal's finances; he himself estimated the net gain at more than £2m. a year, a view widely accepted in spite of scepticism among the directors. A wild boom in East India stock ensued in London, Amsterdam, and Paris. Rich men, including Clive himself, invested in it, while speculators started large-scale dealings in 'differences'. One such group of prominent men was headed by Lord Verney, M.P., Edmund Burke's patron, and included several other M.P.s; and its affairs were managed by two adventurers, William Burke and Lauchlin Macleane, who now began their long and discreditable connexion with Indian affairs. When the directors would not raise the dividend, the 'bulls' set out to obtain a majority in the General Court; split stock and organized an unprecedented publicity campaign; obtained support from deluded proprietors and from the Clive group (which, besides being engaged on the 'bull' side, hoped in the glow of Company affluence to secure an extension of the *jagir* for a further 10 years). The speculators succeeded: in September 1766, the dividend was raised from 6 to 10 per cent.; and they emerged as a new element in Company politics.

Stock-jobbing was at all times in ill-repute with the nation, and the rich, monopolistic Company with the 'popular' party

H

in the City; dislike of Nabobs forcing their way into Parliament and society was growing among the country gentry; and un-easiness was spreading at the 'rapine and oppression' practised in India. The State was grappling with problems of post-war finance, and the question naturally arose what right a trading company had to the territorial revenues of a province subdued with the help of the King's forces. Chatham, in office since July 1766, denied it, and desired a parliamentary inquiry into the Company's affairs as a prelude to State intervention. But his illness, and divisions in his Government, prevented the at-tack from being pressed home, and, after long debates, man-œuvres, and negotiations (for the first time properly elucidated in Miss Sutherland's book), an agreement was reached for two years: the Company undertook to pay the Treasury £400,000 a year. In the meantime the speculators rashly used their majority in the General Court further to raise the dividend from 10 to 12½ per cent. The Government replied with the first parlia-mentary intervention of the century in the internal affairs of the Company: by an Act limiting the dividend to 10 per cent., and another against gerrymandering elections—no one was to vote who had not held his qualification for at least six months. And such intervention had to be continued in order to safeguard the financial interests of the Treasury and of the nation, and to replace the short-term agreement of 1767 by a new settlement. Still, this again was for five years only; the contribution of £400,000 per annum was maintained, but if the Company at any time had to reduce its dividend to 6 per cent. the claim would lapse; the maximum dividend was set at 12½ per cent.

The Act against faggot-votes proved ineffective: operations had merely to start half a year earlier. The opposition in India House, led by Sulivan, was gaining strength, and the election of directors in 1769 was most fiercely contested; the Govern-ment intervened, while groups of rich men recklessly bought up stock at inflated prices. The result was a draw which brought Sulivan back into office. A month later election-mongers and speculators were caught by a sharp break in price caused by news of fighting in India and rumours of an impending French attack: Verney and the Burkes, Sulivan, Macleane, and a great many others were brought to the verge of ruin. But the storm blew over; an attempt of the Government to interfere in the Company's territorial affairs by agents sent out to India ended in failure; and by 1770 a lull supervened in the faction fights at India House, as also in Parliament; during the next two years relations between the Company and the Government were remarkably free of political implications. Meantime information reaching England about Company misrule was producing genuine dismay both in Parliament and in the country, and Sulivan made serious attempts at reform from within. But for this the Company's control over its servants in India had to be strengthened; and moves in that direction were defeated by powerful ex-servants with more than doubtful records. Sulivan's only success was in the remodelling of the Bengal administration, where the man he had chosen, Warren Hastings, laid the basis for Bengal's prosperity under British rule.

But a new crisis in the Company's affairs was impending. High dividends and payments to the Government were based on an illusory surplus from the Bengal territorial revenues. The truth was masked for some time even from the directors, who in March 1771 raised the dividend to 12½ per cent. But even when the situation became clear to them they did not reduce the dividend (which would have stopped also payments to the Government) for fear of a catastrophic break in East India stock, which some of them were heavily 'bulling'. The maximum dividend was continued in August 1771 and March 1772. Then in June a severe financial crisis set in, causing widespread bankruptcies in this country and on the Continent; and now the financial problem of the Company had to be tackled. At first it was hoped that an unspectacular way might be found for the Treasury to help the Company out of its difficulties; but its commitments proved excessive; on 24 September 1772, the half-yearly dividend was passed; and the consequent panic 'raised a frenzy of indignation among shareholders, speculators, and the public at large'. This, on top of the mounting anger of humanitarian opinion, produced a demand for Parliamentary action. The North Administration were forced to evolve an Indian policy.

The view universally held that if the Company were to be helped this must be in return for radical improvements in its organization and rule was grounded 'not only in the desire to obviate financial loss or military danger to the nation but in a wider sense of obligation for law and order in India'. Some favoured the assumption by the Government of full responsibility for the administration of India; but the machinery of government was as yet entirely inadequate for intervention in that distant and unfamiliar field, and the purpose of the temporary settlement embodied in Lord North's Regulating Act of 1773 was 'to leave the Company in control both of trade and day-to-day administration, while checking its worst excesses at home and abroad', and 'to prepare the ground for a more permanent and sweeping reorganization when the Company's charter came up for renewal in 1780'. A small Parliamentary committee was set up of Government supporters, with Jenkinson for *rapporteur*, to examine the Company's books and report on reform. Although its proposals met with considerable opposition, especially in the General Court, the difficulties did not prove insuperable. The Parliamentary Opposition was disunited over India and ineffective; while in India House the Government secured in 1773 a compliant directorate. The Government was ready to help the Company with a loan, and concessions regarding the export of tea; but in three ways established its control over the Company: through the right to receive copies of the Company's accounts and correspondence (henceforth carefully scrutinized by the Secretary of the Treasury, John Robinson); through the nomination of the Governor-General of Bengal and his Council; and through a Government-controlled majority in a reorganized Court of Directors.

....there began...the first period of indirect control by the Government over the East India Company. During this period the 'management' of the Company became one of the regular activities of the Treasury; the King was kept as regularly informed of East Indian elections and of important votes at East India House as he was of the proceedings of Parliament, and there arose to prominence those official experts in Indian affairs of whom Robinson and Jenkinson were the pioneers, and Henry Dundas the most famous.

Here too began the participation of government in the administration of India ... none the worse for basing itself on no particular doctrine of relations of government and Company....

... A step had to be taken that could not be reversed and some of the worst abuses of the Company's rule both in India and at home disappeared for ever....

The Government, 'looking for capacity rather than connexions', appointed Warren Hastings Governor-General, but joined to him three councillors (including the notorious Philip Francis) who within seven days of their arrival launched an attack against him; and from Miss Sutherland's lucid and impartial account of the conflict Hastings comes out much better than his opponents. He was an excellent administrator, absorbed in his work and devoted to duty, and 'widely known among Company servants for his indifference and carelessness about his private fortune'; and though his financial principles hardly 'transcended the conventions of the day, his hands were a good deal cleaner than those of most of his contemporaries': the fortune he amassed was not great by the standards of the time. But the services which he rendered were incalculable: in the circumstances of his last years of office 'it is difficult to think of any other man then concerned in Indian affairs who would have averted disaster.' As for the Parliamentary Opposition, their attitude over those affairs was dictated by personal considerations and the desire to harass the Government. Francis long endeavoured in vain to rouse Burke's concern at the alleged misdeeds of Warren Hastings, and when the Government and the directors decided to recall Hastings, the Rockinghams came out on his side; when Hastings's (ill-chosen) representatives concluded a compromise with the Government, the Rockinghams swung over to the other side; but when Hastings incurred the wrath of the King and the Ministers by refusing to accept that agreement, the Opposition attacks against him stopped abruptly, only to be resumed with increased virulence when he made his peace with the Government.

In the summer of 1778 Robinson started to draft a plan to be followed when in 1780 the renewal of the Company's charter would come up for settlement. While he thought that the Company should resume its contributions to the Exchequer, his experience of the last five years did not make him favour the transfer of the Company's territorial acquisitions to the Government: the change would be dangerous in war-time; the administration of those territories, their commerce, and the remitting of revenue from India were 'greatly connected'; lastly, 'the errors which must be committed in the management of such acquisitions at so great a distance... had better fall upon the directors of the Company than... upon the Ministers of the King'. But while the Cabinet was preoccupied with America and the war, and the Government in a weak position, little progress was made with regard to Indian affairs; the Act of 1773 was renewed for one year, and in May, 1780, for another year. It was not till January 1781, after the Gordon Riots and the General Election, that Indian matters came again to the fore; but even then the strength for decisive measures was lacking. The agreement renewing the charter for 10 years was, in Sulivan's words, 'a paltry performance'; further legislation was vaguely promised. News from India, first of serious conflict in the administration, and next, of military danger in the Carnatic, led to the appointment of two important parliamentary committees. When in February 1781 the Opposition demanded a committee of investigation,

> it did not seem necessary for the Government to oppose it. Carelessness and indifference on North's part, however, permitted... the election of a Committee in which members of the Opposition preponderated both in numbers and quality.... Thus came into existence the famous Select Committee... the field of Edmund Burke's Indian activities.

And in April a secret committee was set up to investigate the causes of the war in the Carnatic; but this time Robinson took care that it should be controlled by the Government side: Dundas was its chairman, with Jenkinson as his right-hand man.

In the two years between the fall of the North Administration and the rise of Pitt, the Indian question became 'one of the major controversies and problems which claimed the attention of Parliament'. Nothing in the terms of reference of either committee suggested that they were intended to formulate general policies of East Indian reform; but under the short-lived Administrations of 1782-4, the two committees became increasingly important, changing their political status several times: the secret committee was connected with the North, Shelburne, and Pitt Administrations, and the select committee with the Rockinghams and the Rockingham Coalition. The Rockingham Administration took no initiative in Indian affairs, and its record was 'somewhat ignominious'. Shelburne inserted in the King's speech of 5 December 1782, a reference to 'fundamental laws' to be framed for India, and Dundas was preparing a Bill (based on the work of Robinson and Jenkinson), which is 'a landmark in the history of Indian legislation', 'the blue-print of Pitt's East India Act of the next year'. Ignoring 'the dislike of the executive characteristic of eighteenth-century political opinion', it proposed to increase the powers of the Governor-General and the Governors; to settle the claims of the rulers of Tanjore and Arcot, and investigate their notorious debts to Company servants; to prevent the General Court from overriding the directors on political matters; and to strengthen the Government in its dealings with the Company. But brought in after the Shelburne Government had fallen, it seemed still-born.

Now the Rockinghams and Burke had their innings. They had long opposed an increase of the authority of ministers over the Company because of the patronage this would give them, and of that of governors as leading to tyranny. Their Bill, which adhered to those tenets, was 'a product of Burke's intelligence', ingenious and unpractical. It was a most sweeping attack on the independence of the Company; the powers, however, and the patronage taken from it were not to be vested in the Crown but in seven commissioners, nominated in the Act for at least four years: that is, in Fox's party whether or not they were in power. Misrule in India was to be checked by a complete subordination of the Indian administrators to commissioners sitting in England—which shows how little Burke understood of the problems of administration. It was a poor Bill, and although its defeat was due to the action of a few resolute men, these were helped by the 'widespread hostility and dislike' which it aroused 'not only among the threatened Indian interests but among a wide body of opinion throughout the country'.

When Pitt in turn introduced his India Bill it was in an understanding with the Company; after what had threatened them they accepted a measure which under normal conditions would have created an uproar. It was Dundas's Bill, modified to meet objections: some of the powers of the Governor-General were dropped, and the extent of the Government's declared patronage was limited. A board, the future Board of Control, was established for India, and measures were enacted against oppression and abuses by the Company's servants.

> What Pitt and Dundas had set out to do was to give themselves both the sanctions and the machinery for carrying out the methods of government supervision and infiltration which North and Robinson had been seeking to employ ever since the Regulating Act of 1773.

And although much remained which called for improvement in Indian administration,

> the confusion of the past twenty-five years had come to an end and a new era had begun in the Government of India and in the relations of State and Company.

9

BASIC FACTORS IN NINETEENTH-
CENTURY EUROPEAN HISTORY

THE TITLE of my lecture seems to call for a closer definition.
The basic factors which I have in mind concern the political
history of Europe in its international aspects during the period
1815–1919, the nineteenth century of European history. That
century and its aftermath witnessed on the Continent the
triumph of linguistic nationality, and of democracy in the sense
of a levelling of classes rather than of constitutional growth;
and it was foremost nationality and the struggles engen-
dered by it that in Central and Eastern Europe defeated the
movement toward self-government and liberty. 'The language
chart is our Magna Charta', was the slogan of nationalism on
the European Continent; and a comparison of the political map
of Europe in 1920, and still more in 1945, with that of 1815
shows that, by and large, the program has been realized, though
hardly with the results its enthusiasts had anticipated: the
operation was successful, but at what cost to the patient? I
propose to examine the patterns that can be discerned in the
seemingly confused historical process which recast the map of
Europe on a linguistic basis. I refrain from inquiring into the
sense of the envenomed struggles we have witnessed; for such
inquiry would take us into inscrutable depths or into an airy
void. Possibly there is no more sense in human history than
in the changes of the seasons or the movements of the stars;
or if sense there be, it escapes our perception. But the historian, when watching strands interlace and entwine and their
patterns intersect, seeks, for the logic of situations and the

rhythm of events which invest them at least with a determinist meaning.

The political problems of the European Continent in the nineteenth century were posed by the French Revolution; and the basic change which it ushered in was the transition from dynastic to national sovereignty, and a progressive widening of the 'political nation' from the privileged orders to democracy, till the nation came to comprise, in theory at least, the entire people. The emphasis of dynastic sovereignty, quasi-proprietary in character, was on the territory of the State; the emphasis of national sovereignty was on the human community—which postulated that a true sense of community should weld the population into one people. From the principle of national sovereignty spring constitutional movements and national demands, claims to self-government and to self-determination. In appearance these had cognate aims, a delusion fostered by their having that common source, and a common opponent in autocracy based on dynastic heritage. In practice, however, there is an antithesis between self-government, which means constitutional development within an existing territorial framework, and self-determination for which there is no occasion unless that framework is called in question and territorial changes are demanded; and acute disputes concerning the territorial framework naturally retard, or even preclude, constitutional development.

In linguistically mixed regions delimitation is a thorny problem even where there is mere juxtaposition of national groups. But in Europe intermixture was as a rule the result of past conquests, political and cultural, which had reduced the original national group to a state of social inferiority. Conquests created Ulsters, and over further, wider regions spread the network of an 'ascendancy' primarily based on the landowning classes and the town population, alien to, or alienated from, the peasantry which retained its own language or religion, or both. Self-government meant, in the earlier stages, the rule of the big landowners and their retainers in the countryside, and of the upper middle class and the intelligentsia in the towns; their language or religion determined the national character of the country (Grattan's Parliament, composed of Anglo-Irish Protestants, deemed itself representative of the Irish nation). Hence in the numerous Irelands scattered all over Europe turmoil and strife were bound to result from the rise of the lower classes, and especially of the peasantry, to political consciousness and action. National and religious conflicts interlocked with agrarian movements, envenoming each other: war was waged for both the national and the personal ownership of the land, and either side felt that it was fighting not for private interests only. An educated upper class, for centuries accustomed to consider the country its own, would not easily allow itself to be reduced to the position of alien interlopers, while peasants rooted in the land, as only they can be, fought the long-drawn battle with an obstinacy unsurpassed by any other class. Moreover the dominant minority invariably had the backings of its Ulster and of its homeland: even under democracy. With the progressive widening of the political nation, the unprivileged orders, one by one down the social scale, were taking over the quasi-proprietary claims of dynasties and feudal oligarchies to territorial dominance; they became ideological partners or heirs of their *quondam* rulers, and frequently their actual partners by being settled on the land or in government posts in the disputed territory. Peasant-settlers planted as a garrison to keep down the subject race, school-teachers sent to spread the language of the minority, and a host of petty officials, constituted a master-nation whose rule was much harder to bear, and more galling, than that of a dynasty or of a remote oligarchy. Consider the amount of disturbance which during the nineteenth century was caused in the political life of this country by an Ireland geographically isolated and not subjected to any further encroachments; and you can gauge the effect which two dozen Irelands were bound to have on the life of nineteenth-century Europe as borderlands between contending nations, especially while attempts continued to be made to complete conquest and conversion.

On the European Continent incomplete conquests fell into two patterns. The main stream of migrations, which had over-run Europe from East to West, was reversed about the eighth

century: from West to East the French pressed against the
Flemings and Germans, the Germans against the Lithuanians
and Slavs, the Lithuanians and Poles against the Russians, and
the Russians against the Finnish tribes, and ultimately also
against the Mongols; each nation was yielding ground in the
West, and gaining much more at the expense of its Eastern
neighbours: in the East were wide spaces and a reduced capacity
for resisting pressure. Similarly the Swedes spread across the
Baltic, and the Italians across the Adriatic. The Flemish-
Walloon problem in Belgium and the Franco-German problem
in Alsace, the numerous problems of Germany's ragged Eastern
border, Poland's problems both on her Western and on her
Eastern flank, and the conflict between the Yugoslavs and the
Italians, all originate in that great West to East shift on the
linguistic map of Europe. The other pattern of conquests whose
consequences were formative of nineteenth-century European
history, goes back to the continued Asiatic incursions, of the
Avars, Magyars, and Turks into South-Eastern Europe. The
Germans met them at the gate of the Danube, between the
Bohemian quadrilateral and the Alps: this is the origin of
Austria whose core was the Ostmark round Vienna, with its
flanking mountain bastions and its access to the Adriatic. Germans and Magyars in their head-on collision split off the
Northern from the Southern Slavs and established their
dominion over that middle zone; and next the subjection of
the Southern Slavs and the Rumans was completed by the
Turkish conquest of the Balkans.

And now compare the political map of Europe in 1815 with
the nationality map which forms the approximate basis of the
frontiers of 1920 and 1945. Practically all the territorial changes
occurred in Central and East-Central Europe. In 1815, the
Germans and the Italians, the two most numerous nations in
that region, were disunited through dynastic fragmentation.
Between them in the West and the Russians in the East, thirteen
to nineteen smaller nations inhabit a belt stretching from Pet-
samo to Candia (their exact number depends on what linguistic
divergences or historical differences are deemed to constitute a
nation): in 1815 all these smaller nations were engulfed in the

Habsburg and Ottoman Empires, in the Eastern fringe of Prussia, and the Western fringe of Russia. But if in that year anyone had attempted to draw a nationality map of Europe, he would have treated Finland as Swedish; the Baltic provinces, all East Prussia and Upper Silesia, and the Czech and Slovene provinces of Austria as German; Lithuania, Latgalia, White Russia, and the Western Ukraine as Polish; practically all Hungary as Magyar; the Austrian Littoral as Italian; and the Christian populations of Turkey possibly as Greek. Thus between the Gulf of Finland and the Turkish border there were only four nations that counted; and in 1848 an educated Englishman discoursing on the rights of nationality would probably be aware of four problems only and of four programs deserving his sympathy: those of German and Italian unification, of Hungary's independence, and of Poland's resurrection (presumably within the frontiers of 1772). As enemies of these programs he would indict the Habsburgs and the Tsar; and if later in the year he heard that ignorant peasantries were fighting on the side of autocracy against those enlightened nations and their eloquent leaders, this would fill him with regret and disgust.

The nationality problem naturally first came up for solution in terms of the master nations; and the main obstacle to three of their four programs was the Habsburg dynasty with its prescriptive rights and policy: of the Polish Question alone, the origin and gravamen lay outside their sphere. No deeper need or conflict had caused Austria's participation in the dismemberment of Poland—only the indiscriminate passion of the Habsburgs for extending their dynastic possessions; and this in time gave rise to schemes for a reconstitution of Poland under Habsburg dominion. Very different was the position of Prussia and Russia with regard to the Polish Question. Geographical consolidation was Prussia's primary purpose in the Partitions: in West Prussia (the 'Corridor' of the inter-war period) there was a conflict between the unity of the seaboard and that of the Vistula river-basin; and in Posnania Polish territory came within seventy miles of Berlin. The Russo-Polish conflict was over White Russia and the Western Ukraine, territories almost twice the size of ethnic Poland, in which the landowners were Roman

Catholic and Polish (or Polonized) while the peasants belonged to the Eastern Churches and continued to speak Russian dialects: the Poles could claim those territories on grounds of nationality so long as peasant-serfs politically counted for little more than cattle; but the frontier attained by Russia in the Third Partition was in 1919 reproduced in the Curzon Line.

One may well ask how in 1795 the Russians came to draw for themselves a frontier correct in the terms of 1919; and the answer sounds even more paradoxical: because they did not think in terms of nationality, or of the political rights of nations as then constituted. They thought in terms of religion, the only ones in which peasant-serfs counted; and by and large religion and nationality coincided. Thus backward Tsarist Russia jumped the period of the master nations, but without being able to destroy the social and economic foundations of the Polish claims to mastery over the disputed provinces: she could not even emancipate the serfs, still less dispossess the big landowners for their benefit, while serfdom and latifundia were maintained in the rest of Russia; nor could the Poles, in 1848 the General Staff of the *sansculottes* of Europe, raise the peasant masses against the Tsarist régime, or they would have destroyed their own hold on those Eastern borderlands. That incongruity of claims and realities, coupled with the impossibility of adjusting them, gave a unique turn to the Polish Question at a time when elsewhere nationality problems were being solved in terms of the socially and culturally dominant nations.

I pass to the alignment of the European Great Powers and the interplay of their interests and policies. What were in 1815 the leading *dramatis personæ* on the European stage? Great Britain and Russia, Powers flanking Europe, in it but never altogether of it, possessed of growing extra-European interests—the rising World Powers; France and Austria, European Great Powers, whose political ambits covered the entire Continent; and Prussia, the least among the Great Powers in size and resources, with limited regional interests and objectives.

Even in 1815 Great Britain and Russia were conscious of their separation from Europe. Next, England expanded into the Second British Empire, which now seems about to combine

with the Western half of the First Empire into an as yet un-
named and ill-defined working community of English-speaking
nations, centring on Washington rather than on London. A
similar shift away from Europe has transferred Russia's capital
from St. Petersburg to Moscow, a distance not to be measured
in miles only, while the centre of gravity of Russia's population
and production has been moving East, toward the Volga and
the Urals. Between 1815 and 1914 the full weight of these two
Powers was seldom felt in Europe, partly owing to the dispersal
or poor organization of their forces, and partly because they
seldom actively intervened in European conflicts except when
the Ottoman Empire was in question, an Asiatic Power which
in the Eastern Mediterranean held the key position between
three continents; and then they were usually ranged on opposite sides. Similarly in the ideological struggle between constitutional systems and autocratic régimes they were opposed to
each other. But three times in 150 years their forces were joined,
first to defeat the French bid for dominion over Europe, and
next the two German bids; and in these German Wars, the
United States started by supporting, and finished by virtually
replacing Great Britain as the flanking Power in the West.
Now the English-speaking nations and the U.S.S.R., engaged
in a contest of global dimensions, can hardly be said to flank
Europe any longer: they face each other in the very centre of
Europe—indeed, what remains of Europe, of its history and its
politics?

On the Continent the game of power politics, in whatever
terms it was played, normally made a neighbour into an enemy,
and therefore the neighbour's neighbour on the opposite flank
into an ally. Hence the rule of odd and even numbers in international politics: if Germany was France's enemy, then Poland
was France's ally, and consequently Russia the ally of Germany
—numbers one and three against two and four; and even sharp
ideological divisions between Germany and Russia could not
prevent that rule from asserting itself in 1922 and 1939. Yet
during the first half of the nineteenth century there was latent,
or even open, hostility between France and Austria which had
no common frontier, while for a century a frontier of more than

500 miles never gave rise to conflict between Prussia and Russia. The intervening numbers in Germany and Italy, whose pressure against France and Austria would have forced them to recognize their common interest, were latent; whereas Prussia and Russia were acutely conscious of their common interest in Poland, the suppressed intervening number—a frontier across territory whose population is alien and hostile to both neighbours is not apt to produce friction between them.

In 1814–15 the Habsburgs withdrew from Belgium and the Rhine, and deliberately divested themselves of responsibility for the defence of Germany; while Prussia, which before 1789 had been primarily an East European, Baltic Power, was entrusted with the 'Watch on the Rhine', and, stretching from Königsberg to the Saar, now covered the entire length of Germany. This redistribution of territory predetermined the ultimate exclusion of Austria from Germany, and Germany's ultimate inclusion in Prussia. But so long as Prussia made the 'Watch on the Rhine' her foremost duty, and *deutsche Treue* toward Austria her leading principle, she was internationally immobilized, and Germany neutralized; and the struggle between France and Austria was carried on across the power-vacuum of Italy. That struggle, begun when Habsburg possessions flanked France both in the East and the West but discontinued during the last thirty-three years of the *ancien régime*, when the Bourbons and the Habsburgs recognized that Great Britain, Prussia, and Russia had become their real rivals, was renewed by the French Revolution and Napoleon, and continued by their epigoni for half a century after 1815.

Austria's existence and Habsburg hegemony over Germany and Italy rested on the principle of dynastic property in States; the presence of the Habsburgs kept the two countries disunited; their disunion secured French primacy in Europe; here was a basis for Franco-Austrian co-operation. But the French flaunted the principle of national sovereignty at Austria: a fit weapon against the Habsburgs, but not an ideological basis for a continuance of French power politics. French statesmen and diplomats from Talleyrand to Thiers were pro-Austrian, but the current of popular feelings ran against Austria—till July 1866 when the cry of *revanche pour Sadowa* resounded on the Paris boulevards: the intervening numbers had emerged. But soon the basis disappeared for a Franco-Austrian alliance. Between 1815 and 1894 France had no ally on the European Continent, and only one constant friend, the Poles, whose friendship was a liability rather than an asset for her; because the implied threat, though never real, tended to draw Russia closer toward Prussia. The co-operation between the Courts of St. Petersburg and Berlin was based on a human affinity between them, on a common autocratic ideology, and on the common anti-Polish interest. Berlin, on the very fringe of German-speaking territory, and St. Petersburg built in Finnish land and given a German name by its Russian founder, stood close to the two ends of the Baltic fringe, territory conquered in the thirteenth and fourteenth centuries by the Teutonic Knights, and ruled until quite recently by their descendants, the Prussian Junkers and the Baltic Barons. These Lutheran Germans, makers and servants of the Tsarist régime, and a power under it, were alien to Slav and Greek-Orthodox Russia, and averse to Pan-Slavism or to constitutional developments which would have endangered their own position. They were anti-Polish and friendly to Prussia; elsewhere they worked the power politics of the Russian Empire, with little distinctive colouring of their own.

The European nationality problems raised in 1848 fell almost all within the ambit of the Habsburg Empire which would have suffered disruption had the programs of the four master nations been realized: Western Austria would have been included in a Greater Germany, and the Czechs and Slovenes engulfed in it; Lombardy and Venetia would have gone to Piedmont; Hungary would have achieved independence, and full dominion over its Slovaks, Yugoslavs, Rumans, and Ruthenes (or Little Russians); over these the Poles would have achieved similar dominion in Galicia. The subject races therefore came out on the side of the dynasty against their social and economic rulers: in order to prevent that rule from being reinforced by political dominion. It was all a phantasmagoria. The Tsar and the King of Prussia still stood by the Habsburgs on grounds of dynastic solidarity; revolutionary forces, which

I

alone could in Germany have cut through the dynastic tangle by proclaiming a Republic one and indivisible, were lacking; the Prussian-Polish conflict in Posnania soon put an end to anti-Russian velleities among the Germans; Piedmont and the Magyars were not a match for the Habsburg Monarchy supported by Russia and the subject races. The transformation, if it was to be, had to be attempted in a different manner.

The Crimean War lost Austria Russia's support; Napoleon III opened up the Italian problem; Bismarck by anti-Polish action in 1863 secured Russia's friendship. In 1859–67, the Habsburg problem was solved in accordance with the modified programs of the master races. The Habsburgs were expelled from Lesser Germany and Italy, but retained the German and Italian provinces which were part of their old hereditary dominions (*Erbländer*); Hungary achieved complete constitutional independence while remaining within the military and international framework of the Habsburg Monarchy; and the government of Galicia was handed over to the Poles. The Austrian Empire changed into the Dual Monarchy, rebuilt on a German-Magyar-Polish basis; and the subject races were delivered to their masters (more completely in Hungary than in Western Austria or Galicia).

In one way Francis Joseph built better than he knew. To the Austrian Germans Western Austria was their heritage, to the Magyars all Hungary, and to the Poles Galicia, and each of these three nations was prepared to fight to the last for every square mile of what it considered its own, while the three heritages together covered the entire Monarchy. No such community of interest could have been found between the dynasty and the subject races. On the other hand, the Emperor's conscious calculations miscarried: he concluded the compromise with the Magyars in the hope of gaining their support for future action against Prussia. In 1870 the Austrian Germans were not willing to fight on the side of France against other Germans, while the Magyars did not wish for a victory which would have re-established the dynastic power of the Habsburgs and might have enabled them to go back on the Settlement of 1867. The logic of the situation defeated Francis Joseph's schemings.

If the struggle for supremacy in Germany could not be resumed any more, a German-Austrian alliance was in the logic
of the situation. Austria-Hungary was surrounded by neighbours each of whom saw populations of his own language within its borders. The Habsburg Monarchy reconstructed on a
German-Magyar basis was a fit ally for Germany, while Germany alone had an interest in its survival, and could therefore
accept an alliance in lieu of complete national reunion (in fact,
Bismarck did not want the Austrian Germans in the Reich,
which inclusion would have unfavourably affected the balance
between the Catholic South and the Prussian North). For
Germany Austria-Hungary was a more convenient ally than
Russia, for in such an alliance Austria-Hungary as the weaker
and more exposed of the two was dependent on Germany,
whereas Germany would have been dependent on Russia.
Moreover Germany had to count with the possibility that the
Power whom she did not pick for ally, would become that of
France; and as such Austria would have been more dangerous
because of the appeal she could make to the Roman Catholic
Germans—Bismarck dreaded a Roman Catholic league against
the Second Reich. Still, Bismarck did not mean to tie Germany
to Austria-Hungary, nor to cut the wire to St. Petersburg. But
again the logic of the situation prevailed: even if Bismarck's
successors had been wise and strong men, it seems doubtful
whether the consequences of an Austrian alliance could have
been permanently avoided. In 1877 Bismarck, when asked by the
Russians what his attitude would be in case of a Russian-
Austrian war, replied that much as he would regret such a
war he could see either side win or lose battles, but not suffer
one of them to be knocked out as a Great Power. Obviously he
feared Germany being left as an isolated intervening number
between two Great Powers, France and Russia or France
and Austria. There was no need for Russia to seek a German guarantee for her existence; there was for Austria. But
once Germany had committed herself to upholding Austria-
Hungary's existence, she was moving from the Baltic fringe
into the Danube Valley and the Balkans; and how long could
the common anti-Polish and reactionary interest preserve

Russia's friendship for a Germany which crossed her path in the Balkans?

Here Russia continued her 'historic mission' of freeing the Greek-Orthodox populations. Of the dominant nations the Turks had the weakest social, economic, and administrative hold over their subject races; even so, the process of destroying the Ottoman Empire in Europe took a hundred years, from the rise of Serbia and the liberation of Greece, across the Russo-Turkish War of 1877–8, to the Balkan War of 1912. But in that process Russia suffered surprises and disappointments; she found Hellenes and Rumans where she had merely seen followers of the Greek-Orthodox Church; and the Bulgars, however pro-Russian in sentiment, from hostility to the Serbs twice joined the Germans in accordance with the rule of odd and even numbers. By 1914 the Balkan nations were free, and the problem of the Greek-Orthodox Serbs and Rumans in the Habsburg Monarchy came to the fore: the survival of the Habsburg Monarchy reconstituted in terms of the dominant nations was now at stake. In 1867, at half-time between Vienna and Versailles, the Austrian Empire changed into the Dual Monarchy; at the close, the Dual Monarchy broke up into the Succession States. But the Russian Empire having collapsed a year earlier, its alien Western fringe, too, disintegrated into national States. The end of the First World War saw the middle zone of the small nations resettled on the basis of linguistic nationality.

In three regions only, socially and culturally dominant minorities retained, or even regained, superiority and possession. The Polish-Masurian fringe of East Prussia and about half of Polish Upper Silesia were left to the Germans on the strength of plebiscites which should never have been held: for there is a nationality *in posse* no less than a nationality *in esse*, and in these territories the process of national revival, universal in Europe, had not yet reached its natural term. On the Adriatic the Italians acquired territory with Yugoslav majorities. And the Poles managed, against the decision of the Allied and Associated Powers, to substitute the Riga for the Curzon Line. All these gains were wiped out by the Second World War. The process which formed the essence of European history since the French Revolution has now reached its term.

Looking back, converted though we cannot be to the *ancien régime*, to the 'system Metternich', or to Tsarism, we no longer exult over the age of nationality and democracy and its victories. All past social superiorities have been wiped out behind the Iron Curtain, and most of the cultural values which the educated classes had created. Anti-Socialist, clerical peasant communities may yet arise in States now satellites of Russia. But a reinstatement of the dispossessed upper and middle classes is impossible. And it is even more idle to think of a reconquest of territories once held on the basis of those lost superiorities. Now territories in Europe can only be regained with 'vacant possession': that is, radically cleared of their present inhabitants. The process of transfers or exchanges of population was started in the Balkans and Asia Minor at the end of the First World War. It was applied by Hitler where it suited him to withdraw German, or expel non-German, populations; and it was planned on an infinitely greater scale by the Germans had they won the war. As they lost it, the process was carried through against them. Hence their wrath.

10

DIPLOMACY IN THE
INTER-WAR PERIOD, *1919-1939*

THE DECLINE in the position and influence of Foreign Ministers and their staffs at the centre, and of their representatives abroad, is the central theme which runs through the collection of essays on *The Diplomats, 1919-1939.*[1]

In Great Britain 'before 1914', writes Professor Craig, 'the right of the Foreign Secretary and the permanent officials of the Foreign Office to consider themselves as the chief advisers of the Cabinet in matters of foreign policy was never seriously questioned'. But after the First World War, 'Foreign Office advice was frequently ignored', and policies were 'adopted by the Prime Minister which ran counter to those advocated by the Foreign Secretary and his staff': important negotiations were taken over by political leaders and their agents, who lacked the necessary training and experience, and this although 'the British foreign service in 1919 compared favourably with that of any other country in Europe'. 'The precedents had been established. In the 1930's ... they were to be improved upon, first by Ramsay MacDonald and later, and more disastrously, by Neville Chamberlain.' Those later developments are only touched upon in a chapter by Professor Gilbert: how Chamberlain (with none of Lloyd George's genius, but even more distrustful of the diplomatic service) would constantly employ emissaries of a very unsuitable kind, and through his confidants maintain 'close relations with the German and Italian Ambas-

[1] Edited by Gordon A. Craig and Felix Gilbert. Princeton University Press.

sadors in London', behind the back of the Foreign Office. At Munich, the chiefs of the other three Governments were accompanied by representatives of their Foreign Offices, but Chamberlain only by Sir Horace Wilson, as unversed as he was himself in international affairs. That nadir of British diplomatic history is not discussed in the book.

'The French Foreign Office', writes Professor Challener, '... emerged from the first world war and the Peace Conference with its prestige undimmed'; 'the vast majority of top diplomatic positions in the French foreign service were held by career men'; and during the seven years of Briand's reign at the Quai d'Orsay, 1925–32, there was close collaboration between him and its Secretary-General, Phillippe Berthelot. The fact that the French nation, in its vulnerable and precarious position, at all times paid attention to foreign policy, upholding its basic traditions, and that the Prime Minister himself frequently held the Foreign Office, added to its strength. Yet there is another side to the picture. At the Paris Conference Berthelot was passed over by Clemenceau who 'preferred to run his own show', and for the same reason the post of Secretary General was left vacant during the thirty months of Poincaré's tenure of the Foreign Office. Nor was Berthelot's régime synonymous with that of the service as such: he had not served outside the Quai d'Orsay since the early years of the century, but, with a group of other *fonctionnaires trop sédentaires*, is alleged to have stood between the ministers and their representatives abroad; similarly his successor, Alexis Léger, after a few years in China, spent the rest of his professional life at the Quai d'Orsay. And when the slide toward appeasement started in French policy, Léger, and with him the Quai d'Orsay, were, as is shown by Miss Cameron, short-circuited by their political chiefs: 'he had no idea of the extent of Laval's private concessions to Mussolini'; in London, after the re-militarization of the Rhineland, he was 'locked out of the decisive conversations', while Flandin 'followed the *politique de complaisance*'; and under Bonnet, in March 1939, Léger found himself 'surrounded with reticence'.

German diplomacy during the inter-war period is dealt with in two essays, by Professor Hajo Holborn and Professor Craig.

In the 1920's, writes Holborn, the regular diplomats 'radiated considerable ill-will toward a republican foreign policy and Ebert at first insisted on Germany being 'represented in eminent diplomatic posts by men who had made their career outside of the German bureaucracy'. None was a failure; and most of them, especially the three Socialist ministers, proved 'unusually effective diplomats'. Yet after 1923 'the restoration of the German professional diplomat was fully achieved', and under Stresemann it was the old guard who dealt with the Western Powers. In relations with Eastern Europe the Foreign Office had a competitor, or rather a pacemaker, in the German army: Seeckt started collaboration with the Soviet Government; the Wilhelmstrasse followed suit, and concluded the Rapallo agreement, well-received by German public opinion as a defiant gesture toward the Western Powers. Nor was that attitude changed by Locarno: in the 'first marked sally of Nazi foreign policy', over the disarmament conference, 'the Foreign Office and the Führer were at one'—Neurath and Bülow, representatives of the old diplomatic service, enthusiastically greeted Germany's break with the Geneva system. In fact, Hitler had his forerunners in the diplomats of the Weimar era; but Holborn, while criticizing the German campaign over the 'war-guilt' clause, omits to add how much the German Foreign Office, with its *Schuldreferat*, was behind it, nor does he mention its concern with the *Auslandsdeutsche*. In ultimate aims there was little to choose between the 'good Germans' and the Nazis; the difference was mainly in tactics and boldness (or rashness): the hesitations or apprehensions of the career diplomats, just as those of the professional soldiers, made Hitler turn elsewhere for advice. 'The Foreign Office', writes Craig,

> was entering an era in which its formerly proud position was to be systematically destroyed ... and ... the Wilhelmstrasse was to be degraded to the role of a mere 'technical apparatus', to carry out decisions in the formulation of which its staff had had no share.

In the very first year of the Nazi régime Goebbels 'annexed most of the staff and the duties of the press section of the Foreign Office'. Next, Ribbentrop established his *Büro* in competition to the official Wilhelmstrasse, and as Special Ambassador negotiated the naval agreement with Great Britain. In 1934, von Papen made his acceptance of the Vienna Embassy conditional upon being 'free from the jurisdiction of the Foreign Office but...responsible to Hitler alone'.[1] Further, Fifth Column operations were entrusted to the *Auslandsorganisation*, which started to make policy on its own. And when Ribbentrop, placed at the head of the Foreign Office, set out to win back for it ground lost to other departments so as to secure its institutional survival, it was 'a survival without meaning', for policy was to be the exclusive concern of Hitler and himself, while the Foreign Office became 'little more than a stenographic bureau': this at least was the line of defence adopted by its officials after the war.

Italian diplomacy during the inter-war period is discussed in two essays by Professors H. Stuart Hughes and Felix Gilbert. There was a conflict between the traditional policy of Italy 'of slow and patient negotiation towards modest goals and the new [Fascist] program of vast ambitions and quick results'. But to begin with the differences were largely 'a matter of vocabulary'. 'Throughout the first decade of Fascist rule, most of the ambassadors continued to be men of the old type, career diplomats and frequently aristocrats.' Even Dino Grandi, 'one of the tough young men of the Fascist movement', when appointed Under-Secretary of the Foreign Office soon came to side with the professional diplomats. Mussolini himself was satisfied with small and cheap triumphs which could be boosted at home: his expansionism was as yet cautious even if his language was

[1] Craig here quotes from Papen's *Memoirs*. But Papen further relates how in 1936 he was saddled with a Counsellor, von Stein, 'an ardent Nazi' who negotiated on his own with the Austrian Nazis and reported direct to the Wilhelmstrasse. Papen refers in particular to one memorandum: 'Its contents have only come to my notice since the war, as part of the collection of German Foreign Office documents published by the Stationery Office in London.' A fine *alibi*—but in fact there is among the German documents a covering note from Papen forwarding that memorandum and commending it as valuable support for a *démarche* of his own. Given due care and caution, German balloons can usually be pricked.

not. When in May 1930, Grandi, now Foreign Minister, pro-
tested against some inflammatory speeches, 'What does it
matter what I say to my crowds?' asked Mussolini. 'Why do
you think I made you Foreign Minister except to be able to talk
here exactly as I please!' But after 1931 revisionism became a
dominant element in Mussolini's foreign policy: in response to
pre-Nazi German revisionism. In 1936 Ciano, who as Minister
of Propaganda had accused the diplomats of pusillanimity and
betrayal of the heroic spirit of the régime, became head of the
Foreign Office; and a year later boasted that it was 'the most
Fascist' Ministry in Italy. Without great changes in personnel,
something had changed in the atmosphere of the Office—'the
clockwork was broken'. The officials no longer knew what was
going on, for all the important work was done in Ciano's
Gabinetto which assumed control over the distribution of in-
coming information. Decisions were now made from above;
'the Ministry existed only to obey', while ambassadors were
poorly informed or briefed. 'Ciano liked to work outside the
regular diplomatic channels. At important embassies he had
confidants'; he also employed special emissaries, and 'cultivated
the method of direct meetings with foreign statesmen'. The
tono fascista in Italian diplomacy pointed to an alliance with
Hitler, and the belief that Mussolini could still be deflected
from it was a fatal delusion fostered in London by the British
Ambassador in Rome, Lord Perth, whom Professor Gilbert
describes as 'one of Britain's most successful and experienced
diplomats'—a statement which hardly does justice to British
diplomacy.

   Soviet diplomacy is discussed in two chapters on Chicherin
and Litvinov by Mr. T. H. von Laue and Professor H. L.
Roberts. The Soviet Government started by abolishing diplomacy: they would address themselves to the peoples rather than
negotiate with Governments which they meant to overthrow.
And though in fact things were to develop along very different
lines, the Foreign Office and its representatives never again
attained real weight or any degree of independence. At the
slightest pretext the Politburo would deal with matters within
the jurisdiction of the Foreign Office; Chicherin, who held it

from 1918 till 1939, ranked low in the Communist party and 'could not expect to be heard in the inner councils'; he rarely dared to assert himself—both at home and abroad the Foreign Office suffered from the competition of the Comintern and the secret police, powerfully represented in the Politburo. Litvinov, an old Bolshevik, was introduced into the office to watch over his chief, before replacing him. But 'the post of the People's Commissar for Foreign Affairs did not, in itself, carry a great deal of weight in the Soviet system', and Litvinov himself did not rank high in the Party. 'Indeed, late in his career he is reported as remarking rather sourly: "You know what I am. I merely hand on diplomatic documents".' The Soviet system and its aims are hardly compatible with any degree of diplomatic autonomy.

The chapters on American diplomacy are of special interest to European readers. The subject is treated in Professor Perkins's chapter on 'The Department of State and American Public Opinion', and in sketches of three American Ambassadors: Dodd by F. L. Ford, and Bullit and Kennedy by William W. Kaufmann. Perkins starts by declaring that 'American diplomatic action has been determined by the people', that 'the general sentiment of the people lies at the root of every great issue', and that Presidents 'have been powerless to withstand these deep-seated feelings'. Are things different in Great Britain or France? And had not Hitler or Mussolini popular feeling behind them? More distinctive is the fact, conditioned by the nature of the American constitution, that in the United States the balance of influence 'is always tipping, . . . now to the executive, now to the legislature, and rarely to the professional diplomat'; and that 'no definite and fixed role can be assigned' to the Secretary of State. The uncertainty of harmony between executive and legislature, the power of Congressional Committees, and the non-Parliamentary position of the Secretary of State, account for some basic differences in the conduct of foreign affairs in the United States and in Great Britain; and in the absence of a deeper integration of the governing bodies, the personality of the President or the Secretary of State is apt to count for more than that of Parliamentary Ministers. American diplomacy in the inter-war period was dominated by the dogma of freedom of action—aloof and ineffective, it was as yet unconscious of the responsibilities of power. The account of the reception given to the honestly meant British inquiry concerning the Geneva Protocal, makes curious reading. And here are the three outstanding cases of active American intervention in world politics during that period: the Four Power pact with regard to the Pacific—'somehow or other ... even in 1922 ... regarded as innocent' (because it applied to the one region in which the United States took an active interest); the Kellogg Pact (even more naive though less mischievous than the League of Nations with which American idealism had burdened Europe); and the naval agreements of 1930 which lulled the United States 'into false security', and compelled the British, 'in order to propitiate the American Government', to reduce cruiser strength, with serious consequences in the 1940s.

Of the three American Ambassadors discussed in this book not one was a career diplomat. William Dodd, sent to Berlin in July 1933, was an ageing historian, who had studied in Germany and who, as so many sentimental pro-Germans, was harking back to 'a Germany that had once been', or that had never been at all. He believed that 'he was to go to Berlin as a living sermon on democracy', and that such an honest, frank mission could hardly fail of good result (consciously austere, he 'never dissembled the hostility he felt toward most career diplomats and businessmen in the Foreign Service'). He practised 'admonition-by-analogy', and found himself disliked in German official circles; and 'once he discovered that he could not convert the Nazis, his despondency practically incapacitated him as a diplomatic representative'. He was a 'worry' for the State Department, and never a key figure in its formulation of policy. Very different was the position of two men with eminently practical experience, Bullit in Paris and Kennedy in London. Their status in the Democratic party and their relations with President Roosevelt (who 'distrusted foreign service officers as a class') gave them a freedom of action not ordinarily accorded to diplomats, and their reports carried, to begin with, considerable weight in Washington, where 'policy was the product of cables received from abroad rather than of a dynamic conception of American interests'. But they, too, lacked an independent approach to the situation. Bullitt, who had long been convinced of the necessity of an agreement with Moscow, having gone there as Ambassador in 1933, returned disgusted and disillusioned, and was henceforth 'dominated by his distrust of the Soviet Union', 'with Great Britain playing the role of minor villain'. Extremely popular in Paris, especially in Government circles, he echoed their views, and played 'minister without portfolio in the kaleidoscope of French cabinets'. Similarly Kennedy in London became an intimate of Chamberlain and his circle, and an appeaser at any price. In short, both took their cues from the governments to which they were accredited, and their influence in Paris and London merely helped to 'reinforce the views already held by Daladier and Chamberlain'. After Munich Bullitt perceived at last the full extent of the German danger and at the time of the collapse of France played a part which did him credit (though even then he was capable of suspecting Britain of conserving her 'air force and fleet as bargaining counters for future negotiations with Hitler'). Kennedy, on the other hand, remained convinced that the United States must keep out of the conflict whatever may happen, and that England 'will go down fighting' but that it will not do 'the slightest bit of good'. He became 'a prophet of unrelieved gloom' and inaction, and lost all influence with the President. Both failed in their mission; they 'could obtain little or no guidance from the State Department', and gave it as little in return. But could they not find 'a fund of knowledge and experience' with the staffs of professional diplomats by whom they were served? Kaufmann's conclusion is that they could not, and that most of their faults derived 'from the sterility which characterized the thought of the professional diplomat during the inter-war period'. The book closes by registering insufficiency at all levels.

About a hundred years ago Guizot wrote in his *Mémoires*:[1]

The professional diplomats form, within the European community, a society of their own which lives by its own principles,

[1] Vol. ii, pp. 266–7.

customs, lights, and aspirations, and which, amid differences and even conflicts between States, preserves a quiet and permanent unity of its own. Moved by the divergent interests of nations, but not by their prejudices or momentary passions, that small diplomatic world may well recognize the general interest of the great European community with sufficient clearness and feel it with sufficient strength, to make it triumph over differences, and cause men, who have long upheld very different policies without ever quarrelling among themselves, and who have almost always shared the same atmosphere and horizons, to work sincerely for the success of the same policy.

The picture may be somewhat idealized but is not altogether fanciful. That diplomatic community had for its background the great French-speaking 'international' of the European aristocracy, which Guizot, French but not an aristocrat, diplomat but not *de carrière,* beheld with perhaps excessive admiration during years influenced by Princess Lieven. Now it is gone, and nothing can re-create it; and whatever of it had survived into the present century, was apt to rouse the ire, first of 'democrats' prating about 'open diplomacy' and 'diplomacy by conference',[1] and next of the dictators; and besides, the disapproval of a good many who fall into neither category. Distrust of professional diplomats is registered in almost every single chapter of this book.

But were a book attempted on the generals of the period, a similar story would be told. Clemenceau is credited with the

---

[1] Professor Craig touches upon the activities of that egregious group in Great Britain which, in the first quarter of this century, went by the name of Union of Democratic Control, and seems to overrate its importance. As *finale* to its activities he might have quoted the *démarche* undertaken on 29 July 1939, by one of its last survivors, Charles Roden Buxton, who told the Counsellor of the German Embassy that public discussion of how to preserve peace could 'no longer achieve its purpose', and that it was 'necessary to revert to a sort of secret diplomacy', and seek a way out of the difficulties 'by conversations from which the public was totally excluded'. In short all that was left of the *credo* of the U.D.C. was a pathetically naive belief in their own fitness to conduct diplomatic negotiations. (See *Documents and Materials relating to the Eve of the Second World War,* published by the Ministry of Foreign Affairs of the U.S.S.R., vol. ii, *Dirksen Papers,* pp. 106–12).

dictum that the conduct of war is too serious a business to be left to generals; others too, have acted on that principle. The man who bears the supreme responsibility in the State must retain the supreme direction of its most vital business: of home policy in peace time; of diplomacy in times of crisis; and of operations in war. So did monarchs in past ages; and so do modern heads of the Executive. And in this century international affairs so much dominate the life of the nations that the direction of foreign policy cannot be left to experts nor even to departmental chiefs, but must become the attribute of Presidents, Prime Ministers, or dictators: if ill-chosen, the worse for those who place them in positions of supreme power. But outside interference with the work of professionals, however authoritative, is apt to cause friction; and then the man at the top is likely to look for tools of his own: which adds to the difficulties of the situation. Still, in spite of a few outstanding men such as Rumbold, Coulondre, or Schulenburg, the diplomats, especially during the second half of the inter-war period, seem to have been hardly better fitted to deal with the situation than were their chiefs. There was insufficiency at all levels. There may have been in Europe an all-round decline during the inter-war period caused by human losses suffered in the war, and by deep disturbances of the mental and moral atmosphere among the survivors. Or perhaps the complexities of man-created problems now transcend the capacities of man with consequencies rendered even more serious by the steady growth of his technical power.

2

The European situation during the inter-war period turned on the same two pivotal problems with which we are now faced once more: of German nationalism and Russian Bolshevism, and how to contain one without playing into the hands of the other. The capacity of either for military renascence was vastly underrated, and so was their capacity for co-operating despite ideological differences and a cordial mutual dislike. The frontiers of Germany as drawn at Versailles were eminently fair to the Germans: France gave in over the Rhineland and even over the Saar; and plebiscites were held in East Prussia and Upper Silesia where the Polish national revival was advancing without having reached its term. Still, the Germans kept up a spurious agitation over the Corridor and Danzig; while the Sudetens, Pan-Germans in 1848 and forerunners of the Nazis in 1898, could be trusted to reject even a Swiss settlement with the Czechs (a *Verschweizerung* Henlein contemptuously called it in 1937). How then could the national existence of Poland and Czechoslovakia be safeguarded except through a French hegemony in Europe? And how could French hegemony be maintained without restrictions on German sovereignty and armaments? The triple failure of French, Czech, and Polish diplomacy, working on different lines, forms a curious pattern in the book on *The Diplomats*.

Could the policy of Clemenceau and Poincaré toward Germany have been carried through, as that of containing France was after the Treaty of Vienna, Europe might have been spared a new deadly dose of German aggression. It was abandoned by the French themselves: French humanitarian liberalism was averse to indefinitely holding down the Germans; there was the old, deep-rooted pacifism both of the French *haute finance* and of the French labour movement, and a widespread fear and dislike of Russian Bolshevism; a horror at the idea of another war, and a weakening of the French national fibre; hence an exaggerated regard for British and American opinion: a nation which abandons safeguards essential to its own security in deference to foreign opinion ceases indeed to be a Great Power. Whatever the reasons, there was French *défaillance* after 1925: disguised at first, stark in its concluding stages; and the action of French diplomacy toward Germany during those fourteen years was almost invariably softer than its professions.

The French system as planned in 1919 attached considerable importance to the alliances with Poland and Czechoslovakia, 'partners in the job of holding Germany in check'; and Philippe Berthelot, the Secretary General of the Quai d'Orsay, was their 'most consistent artisan'. Yet he was opposed to the Ruhr occupation, being convinced 'that, somehow or other, Germany and France must manage to live together in the same

European system', or the weight of 70 million organized hard-working Germans would ultimately prove too much for 38 million Frenchmen: 'if . . . we don't try to create a German republic hostile to war, we are doomed'. The fact which neither he nor other advocates of reconciliation with Germany would squarely face was that a free hand toward Poland was Germany's irreducible price for friendship with the West: otherwise she would seek and find her natural ally against the Poles in Russia. Briand's guiding rules for French diplomacy, 'to insure for France . . . all possible elements of immediate security . . . and in rhythm with its development, to seek the broader bases of European peace', sound well so long as no attempt is made to translate them into concrete terms. How could close Anglo-French co-operation and a Franco-German rapprochement be reconciled with Eastern alliances in which Great Britain refused to participate and which the Germans were out to annul? Locarno drew a clear distinction between Germany's Western and her Eastern frontiers; but an attempt was immediately made to obscure it by making Germany conclude arbitration treaties with Poland and Czechoslovakia, which neither reassured the Poles nor were ever taken seriously by the Germans.

The Locarno treaties were well-nigh symbolic of the self-deceiving diplomacy of the League of Nations period. Berthelot, according to his friend Claudel, 'put the Locarno program into effect and between 1925 and 1932 went along with Briand not so much because he believed in the policy but simply because he could envisage no alternatives'. In fact Locarno was an abdication on the part of France: 'the French never again would act alone', writes Challener; 'they had . . . lost a large part of their nerve. . . .' To the Germans, on the other hand, it was a mere starting point. 'What was so alarming', wrote Alexis Léger, 'was that it seemed impossible to reach finality; each concession, freely granted in the desire to conciliate, was promptly followed by fresh and yet more extravagant demands.'[1] Briand died in

[1] Cf. also Rumbold's despatch of 3 July 1930: 'It is an unattractive feature of the German character to display little gratitude for favours received, but when the receipt of favours is followed up by fresh demands, there are grounds for feeling impatient.'

K

1932, before the bankruptcy of his policy had become blatantly obvious. Berthelot, unnerved by the impact of failure, 'isolated himself more and more in the accomplishment of his purely routine, administrative tasks'; and a short time before his death, bitterly remarked that the law of gangsters was being imposed everywhere, and that 'brigands have more energy than honest men'.

By 1935 the growing weakness of France was patent, and led to an independent policy on the part of Poland, which in turn still further undermined the French system. There were only two logical lines which French policy could have now pursued: to contain Hitler Germany through an alliance with Soviet Russia, even if this was to estrange Poland still further; or to adopt a policy of *rapprochement* with Germany tacitly sacrificing her Eastern allies. Both these policies were attempted, without ever being fully avowed or carried through to their distasteful end. M. Coulondre, the outstanding French diplomat in the last years of the inter-war period, though under no illusions as to the character and ultimate aims of the Soviet Government, 'clung with dogged consistency to two simple ideas: first, that Germany must be stopped; second, that only a tight military alliance between the Western Powers and the Soviet Union could stop her'. And he clearly realized that Czechoslovakia was 'the only country on which the action of the three great peaceful Powers could be conjoined'. He also saw that, especially in view of Poland's expansion beyond the Curzon Line, no such junction could be expected for her defence, and he did not overestimate, as many did, her military importance. But he was 'The Voice in the Wilderness'—the title of the essay about him which Mr. Ford and Professor Schorske contribute to the book.

A more comprehending reception was given in the Laval-Flandin-Bonnet period to the policy advocated by M. François-Poncet, whose career is sketched in Mr. Ford's essay on 'Three Observers in Berlin'. François-Poncet started as a scholar and teacher; during the war of 1914 turned to applied economics; through his marriage 'acquired substantial holdings in the steel industry'; during the Ruhr occupation was economic adviser to the commanding general; sat in the Chamber of Deputies, 1924–31, 'a skillful opponent of organized labour and one of French industry's cleverest parliamentary spokesmen'; in 1930 was appointed Under-Secretary at the Quai d'Orsay, and next in the Premier's office under Laval; and in 1931, at the age of 46, was sent as Ambassador to Berlin. While inclined to be tough toward Weimar Germany, he always favoured closer industrial ties between Germany and France, and even before he went to Berlin, 'had proposed a complex international cartel plan'. He soon came to doubt the chances of blocking Hitler by frontal resistance, and anyhow would only have attempted it with Mussolini for ally: he openly showed to the Germans his dislike of the Spanish government, 'this last stronghold of the Popular Front', and of the French-Soviet pact of 1935.

> The policy for which François-Poncet was agitating, once identified beneath the disavowals that burden his *Souvenirs* . . . was, in fact, the common property of a substantial section of the French Right. Fear of the Russia of Stalin, indifference towards the Czechoslovakia of Beneš, reliance on the Poland of Beck, admiration for the Italy of Mussolini, all were implicit in the ambassador's attitude. . .

'It is time', he said to Neville Henderson in May 1938, 'that Europe revised its opinion of M. Beneš'; and to Sir Eric Phipps, Ambassador in Paris, early in June, 'that the Allies should offer Hitler a deal on the Sudeten question'. Soon he was urging 'the possibility of a Great Power settlement and "evolutionary changes" in existing alliances'; and 'the vital preparatory work' for Munich was carried out by him in a visit which, on orders from Bonnet, he paid to Hitler on the morning of 28 September —but the 'ambassador's memoirs tend to minimize his own importance in this instance, stressing instead the decisive role of British policy throughout the crisis'. And next, he made his 'culminating effort to achieve better relations between Paris and Berlin': during his visit to Berchtesgaden on 18 October, he broached the idea of the Franco-German declaration, signed on 6 December during Ribbentrop's visit to Paris. But by that time François-Poncet had left Berlin 'to take up his duties in

Rome, where he remarked to the German Ambassador that it had been time for him to leave the Reich: "You should stop while it tastes best".' In Rome he declared to Mussolini 'that "he had come to develop the policy of the Munich Agreement" by converting into reality the dream of a four Power system'. He certainly did not relish the crudities of the Nazi régime, yet 'nothing about Nazism so repelled him as to inhibit his efforts to arrange an understanding between the French government and French industry, on the one hand, and Hitler's Reich, on the other'; and in Rome 'he was willing to swallow the insults he received', and still pursue his European plans based on business pacifism.

It was possible, though hardly sensible, to imagine that France could achieve security behind a military and diplomatic Maginot line; but in the case of Czechoslovakia and Poland geographical situation and ethnic composition alike precluded isolation. The basic factor in the national restoration and the national survival of both was their alliance with France: yet even this failed to create any real community between the Czechs and the Poles. On the German front there was a fine but significant difference between them: Austria was the old enemy of the Czechs, but Prussia of the Poles; elsewhere their hostilities and policies diverged still more. Besides, in outlook and traditions, based on widely different social structures, the two nations were unsympathetic to each other; and the conflict over Teschen was merely a symptom of a much deeper cleavage. Both States bore the imprint of their makers, Masaryk and Pilsudski; and the two found their disciples and heirs in Beneš and Beck who, especially after the deaths of their masters, were in complete control of the foreign policies of their States.

'Czechoslovakia: The Diplomacy of Eduard Beneš' is the title of Mr. Paul Zinner's essay. Indeed, during the twenty years of Czechoslovakia's independent existence, her foreign policy was made by Beneš who became 'Foreign Minister by profession'. As such he combined expert knowledge derived from long practice with 'a general disdain for expert advice and a penchant for informal diplomacy' which he practised travelling as 'a roving ambassador of his country' from one European capital to another and to Geneva, in 'an attempt to deal with the responsible European statesmen personally...' He 'clearly saw that the welfare of a democratic Czechoslovakia coincided with the maintenance of a stable and peaceful Europe', of the Versailles *status quo* and the effectiveness of the League of Nations system. His foreign policy was a continual search for security, both through bilateral and regional agreements—the French alliance and the Little Entente—and through general schemes of arbitration and pacific settlement of disputes. He tried assiduously to increase the moral and political prestige of the League, and within the League he vindicated the rights of the lesser European Powers: among their representatives he 'perhaps stands out as the one who was most often and most intimately involved in events of European significance'. Truly conciliatory, a believer in Parliament and Assemblies, always keen to explain his thought and to discuss compromises, an enthusiastic supporter of any scheme aiming at collective security, he was listened to with attention in the 1920's, but with growing impatience in the changed international climate of the 1930's: 'his old gifts had little relation to the realities of the new age of power politics'. When the crisis came of Czechoslovakia's existence Beneš's alliances and treaties proved mere scraps of paper, and his League concepts idle dreams; and he was run down, derided, and traduced. 'Diplomacy by conference' used Geneva phraseology in its Munich performance; and Beneš, who had so long employed it, believing or wishing to believe in the shams of the League, was in the end unable to face stark reality and capitulated, rather than take the risk of single-handed action. Even Czechoslovakia's re-establishment after the war could not repair the loss of prestige which he had suffered through his surrender in 1938. It was a contributing factor to his second and final defeat in 1948.

Masaryk was of humble origin, a scholar and thinker with a humanitarian outlook; Pilsudski, of gentry extraction and a revolutionary conspirator and terrorist by early training, was a bold and bitter fighter, contemptuous of other men, and scornful of Parliamentary institutions and public opinion. Beneš and Beck both tried to walk in the paths of their masters; but to fall short in philosophical elevation is far less pitiable than to flop as the strong man; and as Mr. Henry Roberts says of Beck, 'this . . . rather Mephistophelean figure conveyed an impression of hardness without depth'. When disaster overwhelmed him, he received scant sympathy, and is remembered

> as the man who refused to work with the Little Entente or the League of Nations, who pursued, in substance, a pro-German policy after 1934, who joined in the dismembering of Czechoslovakia, and, finally, as the man whose stubborn refusal to enter any combination with the Russians contributed to the failure of the Anglo-French-Soviet negotiations of the spring and summer of 1939.

Beck's manner of doing things, with a gratuitous display of arrogance and brutality, and by temperamental reaction rather than to rational purpose, put an unpleasant complexion even on policies not lacking deeper justification. Doubts might well have been entertained concerning the League; still, it was not for Poland in her precarious situation to try to impair its authority, from sheer resentment at the 'minority treaties' and League control in Danzig. The Little Entente was directed against the Magyars, a gentry nation like the Poles and their traditional friends; and while to the Czechs Russia was their 'big brother', to Poland, in possession of White Russian and Ukrainian lands, she was a dangerous enemy. France expected unquestioning devotion from the Poles, but at Locarno concluded an equivocal treaty with the Germans, after that attempted an Eastern Locarno with the Russians, and throughout displayed weakness toward Nazi Germany. No wonder if the Poles tried to re-insure themselves in their own fashion. Beck's action towards Czechoslovakia was mean, brutal, and stupid, but it hardly became French Munichers to rate him for it. In 1939 the Western Powers ought perhaps to have sacrificed Poland to Russia; but the Poles could not be expected to do so themselves. Mr. Roberts, while admitting certain criticisms of Beck, says that 'in all probability no arrangement by the Eastern European States could have assured the security of the area, even had their statesmen been far wiser and more self-restrained'; and Mr.

Zinner, speaking about Czechoslovakia's paper alliances, questions 'whether an alternate course of action by Beneš . . . would have been crowned with greater success'. There are situations wherein it is well-nigh impossible for statesmen or diplomats to be justified by results.

II

'HITLER: A STUDY IN TYRANNY'

MUST WE talk of Hitler? We must, however distasteful the subject: for a reckoning there has to be with the forces that made
him, and we shall have to reckon with them also in the future:
and the viler Hitler the man, the more significant is the part
which he was able to play in history. The first thing therefore is
to have the facts about him carefully sifted, soberly stated, and
properly documented: this Mr. Alan Bullock has done in the
730 pages of his book, *Hitler: A Study in Tyranny.* He does not
attempt ingenious explanations, which would unavoidably
result in a one-sided selection and grouping of material: scope
is left to the judgement of the reader. I shall try to delineate
some of the essential features of Mr. Bullock's story.

Adolf Hitler, born in 1889 the son of a petty Austrian official,
refused to follow his father's profession. 'One day it became
clear to me', he writes in *Mein Kampf*, 'that I would be a
painter, I mean an artist. . . .' Note how he guards against
being misunderstood: an artist, not a house-painter. He speaks
of the deep ditch that separated the *petit bourgeois*, 'among
whom I passed my younger days', from the working classes;
'this division,' he says, 'which we may almost call enmity',
springs from fear of reverting to the condition of manual lab-
ourers, or at least of being classed with them; and he himself,
in his passionate refusal to join a trade union, reproduced that
attitude. At the climax of his career Hitler still thought that
he should have been a great painter or architect and not a statesman. But he had neither artistic taste nor ability and, in spite of
training received at an art school in Munich (an episode left

out of *Mein Kampf*), he failed to secure admission to the Vienna Academy of Fine Arts. Unwilling to settle down to regular work, lazy and moody, he became a social nondescript: he slept in doss-houses, did casual jobs, or painted picture post-cards or posters and advertisements for small shops. But all along his passion was reading newspapers and talking politics, which even then he did with uncontrolled violence. 'He gave rein to his hatreds—against the Jews, the priests, the Social Democrats, the Habsburgs.... The few people with whom he had been friendly became tired of him, of his strange behaviour and wild talk.' 'During these years', writes Hitler, '... a defin-ite outlook on the world took shape in my mind. ... Since then I have extended that foundation very little, I changed nothing in it...'—which was only too true. Mr. Bullock repeatedly adverts to the Austrian strands in Hitler's character and men-tality; he was truly representative of his class and country, and especially of that unadulterated provincial Austria with its surly hostility to Imperial, cosmopolitan Vienna and its Jewish intel-ligentsia. 'It is not by the principles of humanity that man lives', declared Hitler in February 1928, '... but solely by means of the most brutal struggle.' This Mr. Bullock describes as 'the natural philosophy of the doss-house'. But there is another, per-haps more significant, side to it: after 1866 and 1870, German nationalists in Austria had come to worship Prussia's strength; of the positive qualities from which it sprang—hard work, mental tidiness, devotion to duty, regularity, and an austere (though very narrow) morality—they had none, least of all Hitler, nor could he have acquired them; what such a sham-Prussian could reproduce on the cheap was brutality.

Hitler left Vienna in 1913, perhaps to evade military service for which he failed to report. In 1914 he joined the German Army: war was to him an escape from frustration and failure. In December 1914 he was awarded the Iron Cross, Second Class, and in August 1918, the Iron Cross, First Class, 'an uncommon decoration for a corporal'. Neither the reason of that award, nor of his remaining a corporal, has been satisfactorily ex-plained. At the end of the war Hitler was in his thirtieth year; he had little prospect of finding a job; in fact, 'he was not interested in work. . . ; he never had been': 'I resolved', he writes, 'that I would take up political work.' What part he played, if any, during the Munich Communist régime of April–May 1919, is uncertain. After its overthrow, Bavaria, under a right-wing government with strong particularist leanings, became the refuge of shady elements from the late Freikorps, bitter enemies of the Weimar régime, and a training school for political murder and terrorism; the Police President of Munich, when asked if he knew that there were political murder gangs in Bavaria, replied: 'Yes, but not enough of them.' Similarly minded, Major-General von Epp of the Munich Army Command, and his Assistant, Major Roehm, gave Hitler in its Political Department the post of educational officer for the troops 'with the task of inoculating the men against contagion by socialist, pacifist or democratic ideas'. Into the German Workers' Party which Hitler was building up, Roehm pushed ex-Freikorps men and ex-servicemen; and the first 'strong arm squads' were formed under an ex-convict, the nucleus of the S.A. Hitler was now able to prove his powers of agitator and mob orator, and under protection from the Army Command to form and practise with impunity his methods of incitement, violence, and intimidation.

In a speech of 30 January 1941, Hitler claimed: 'No human being has declared or recorded what he wanted more often than I'—nor his methods: few politicians have made known with equal frankness their views about the masses and how to appeal to them. Their receptive powers 'are very restricted', Hitler wrote in *Mein Kampf*, 'and their understanding is feeble . . . all effective propaganda must be confined to a few bare necessities and . . . expressed in a few stereotyped formulas'. 'The broad masses of the nation . . . more readily fall victims to the big lie than to the small lie, since they themselves often tell small lies in little matters, but would be ashamed to resort to large-scale falsehoods.' 'The masses feel very little shame at being terrorized intellectually and are scarcely conscious of the fact that their freedom as human beings is impudently abused.' 'The very first condition . . . in every kind of propaganda is a systematically one-sided attitude towards every problem that has to be dealt with. . . . When they see an un-compromising onslaught against an adversary, the people have at all times taken this as proof that right is on the side of the active aggressor . . .' 'The art of leadership consists of consolidating the attention of the people against a single adversary. . . . The leader of genius must have the ability to make different opponents appear as if they belonged to one category.' Here then were in a nutshell the precepts of the supreme political gangster with an insight bordering on genius into the psyche of his own nation: the crass immorality of his tenets and methods shocked few among the Germans who have long relished an ostentatiously cynical attitude in politics; and whatever was offensive in his pronouncements, each would only apply to the others.

Hitler had no use or respect for truth, hardly any conception of it. The mental processes of criticism and analysis jarred on him, and his hostility to 'freedom of thought or discussion represented a personal dislike quite as much as a political expedient'. He talked incessantly, and with a blend of fanaticism and calculation would talk himself into conviction or 'whip himself into a passion which enabled him to bear down all opposition, and provided him with the motive power to enforce his will on others'. 'The most obvious instance of this', writes Mr. Bullock, 'is the synthetic fury, which he could assume or discard at will, over the treatment of German minorities abroad.' He would not listen to the Germans in the South Tyrol and helped to uproot them in the Baltic States, but worked himself into a frenzy of indignation over imaginary persecutions in Czechoslovakia or Poland when he wished London or Paris to soften up for him the victim he was about to attack. 'Hitler in a rage appeared to lose all control of himself. His face became mottled and swollen with fury, he screamed at the top of his voice, spitting out a stream of abuse, waving his arms wildly and drumming on the table or the wall with his fists. As suddenly as he had begun he would stop, smooth down his hair, straighten his collar and resume a more normal voice.' There was 'skilful and deliberate exploitation of his own temperament.'

He hit, according to Mr. Bullock, on a psychological fact (certainly true of the Germans): 'that violence and terror have their own propaganda value, and that the display of physical force attracts as many as it repels'. In using violence Hitler would give it the widest possible publicity. 'The reputation of our hall-guard squads', he wrote in *Mein Kampf*, 'stamped us as a political fighting force and not as a debating society.' In his speeches he stressed and repeated such words as 'smash', 'force', 'ruthless', or 'hatred'; and his shortcoming as an orator 'mattered little beside the extraordinary impression of force, the immediacy of passion, the intensity of hatred, fury, and menace conveyed by the sound of the voice alone without regard to what he said'. 'With an almost inexhaustible fund of resentment in his own character to draw from', he made the appeal to nationalist resentment an essential part of his stock-in-trade, and offered the Germans 'a series of objects on which to lavish the blame for their misfortunes'. 'Lashing himself to a pitch of near-hysteria, he would scream and spit out his resentment', evoking a hysterical response in his audience. Otto Strasser, one of his bitterest critics, wrote:

> Adolf Hitler enters a hall. He sniffs the air. For a minute he gropes, feels his way, senses the atmosphere. Suddenly he bursts forth. His words go like an arrow to their target, he touches each private wound on the raw, liberating the mass unconscious, expressing its innermost aspirations, telling it what it most wants to hear.

And Hitler himself says about the orator: 'He will always follow the lead of the great mass in such a way that from the living emotion of his hearers the apt word which he needs will be suggested to him and in its turn this will go straight to the hearts of his hearers.' There is a Jewish legend that the burning bush, from which the voice of the Lord spoke to Moses, was the nation of Israel gathered at the foot of Mount Sinai. The wording of the *Declaration of the Rights of Man and Citizen*, over which the most distinguished draftsmen had floundered in the seclusion of their studies, came to them, lapidary and noble, as they were facing the crowded Assembly. And it was again on the masses that Hitler drew: what was worst in the Germans, their hatreds and resentments, their envy and cruelty, their brutality and adoration of force, he focused and radiated back on them. A master in the realm of psyche but debarred from that of the spirit, he was the Prophet of the possessed; and interchange there was between him and them, unknown between any other political leader and his followers. This is the outstanding fact about Hitler and the Third Reich.

Hitler made also a tactical discovery: that it was possible in Germany to create a mass-organization comprising hundreds of thousands of armed men, to extol its 'indomitable aggressive spirit' and its determination brutally to enforce its will, and yet play safe. The S.A., says Mr. Bullock, was for street brawls only, 'the shock troops of a revolution that was never to be made': Hitler was determined to obtain power 'without a head-on collision with the forces of the State, above all with the Army'. On May Day 1923, 20,000 armed Stormtroopers were gathered in a field near Munich for an attack against the Socialist procession; but when a thin cordon of troops was thrown round them, Hitler, though urged by some of his lieutenants to use his superior numbers to overpower the troops, capitulated. That no further action was taken against him by the Bavarian Government and the Army 'suggested that, in more favourable circumstances, another attempt to force the hand of the authorities might succeed'. It was indeed with their help that, half a year later, he hoped to pull off his *Putsch*. But he bungled the affair, and would have withdrawn once more had not Ludendorff forced him to act. They marched the next morning, were met by a line of police, and were fired at; Ludendorff and his A.D.C. pushed through the line, but the Nazi leaders, who had all the time 'appealed openly to violence, crumpled up and fled', Hitler first. 'His revolution—even in 1923—had been designed', writes Mr. Bullock, 'as a "revolution by permission of the Herr President"'; and proposals to have him deported—he was still an alien—were shelved by indulgent protectors in high places.

Never again was he to risk a collision with the armed forces of the State: when in 1925 he was forbidden for a time to speak

in public, he obeyed; and when in April 1932, the dissolution
was ordered of the S.A., by then 400,000 strong, and Roehm
thought of resisting, Hitler insisted that the S.A. must obey.
Revolutionary action as he understood it, that is violence on a
grand scale, had to be postponed till he was invested with the
power of the State and in control of its machinery (but when
five Nazis in the Silesian village of Potempa kicked to death a
Communist in front of his mother, he addressed them as 'My
comrades', and told them that their liberation was 'a question
of our honour'). In Parliamentary and Presidential elections he
engaged under protest: 'For us Parliament is not an end in itself, but merely a means to an end . . . we are a Parliamentary
party by compulsion . . . democracy must be defeated with the
weapons of democracy.' But once he was able to do so constitu-
tionally, he would form the State in the manner he thought
right; and then, he added, 'heads will roll': a prospect which
was apparently cheering rather than repellent to the ever-
growing throng of his followers.

Within the Party, the Führer insisted on unquestioning sub-
mission to his will and commands: disobedience was the only
'moral turpitude' punished with expulsion from the Party.
Discipline heightened in individual members the feeling of
aggregate strength; and the Party program was declared unalterable, and was never allowed to become a subject of discussion. 'But the attitude of the leaders towards the program',
writes Mr. Bullock, 'was entirely opportunist. For them . . . the
real object was to get their hands on the State. They were . . .
the gutter *élite*, avid for power, position, and wealth. . . .' Hitler
would adjust his program to suit his audience. 'The Communists deliberately limited their appeal to one class, while
Hitler aimed to unite the discontented of all classes.' Much of
his following still adhered to anti-capitalist tenets, but he was
building up the movement on large subsidies from the political
funds of the heavy industry and big business. Conservative
politicians and the generals had control of the State and the
Army, and the bankers and business men had the money; but
Hitler had the masses. While they carried on government by
Presidential decrees and with dwindling popular and Parlia-

mentary support, he, in the Reichstag elections of July 1932, secured nearly 14 million votes, 37·3 of the total cast. The question was when the two sides would join hands, and on what terms. In the end Hitler attained power not through a clear electoral majority, nor through an irresistible revolutionary or national movement: 'he was jobbed into office by a backstairs intrigue', writes Mr. Bullock, 'by a shoddy deal with the "Old Gang".' Yet his power 'was founded on popular support to a degree few people cared, or still care, to admit', and he made a genuine appeal, especially to the younger generation. Moreover millions of non-Nazis showed no moral repugnance to him and his methods; and, what mattered most, he was favoured by the Army and its leaders.

The Conservative politicians who had placed him in office and joined him in it, believed that he could be held in check and tamed. They were soon left gasping for breath. He was free of all restraint or inhibitions in using the formidable power placed in his hands, 'a man without roots, with neither home nor family', writes Mr. Bullock, '... who admitted no loyalties, was bound by no traditions, and felt respect neither for God nor man.' Conscience was to him 'a Jewish invention, a blemish like circumcision', and Providence was invoked only as a foil to his own person. He boasted. 'We have no scruples, no bourgeois hesitations'; he combined considerable intellectual powers and a political virtuosity; and he was now ruler of a nation which, like himself before he had attained power, would duly submit to any decree of those placed in authority over it. Step by step he achieved arbitrary power, more absolute even than that of Mussolini. All political landmarks were eliminated in the German scene; the Federal States, the political parties, the Trade Unions, were annihilated in the process of *Gleichschaltung*. The Civil Service and the police were purged; the spoils of office went to the Nazis. 'The street gangs', writes Mr. Bullock, 'had seized control of the resources of a great modern State'. From the first the Jews were delivered to merciless persecution, and violence and cruelty were encouraged against previous opponents. There was a breakdown of law and order with the connivance of the State. 'Men were arrested, beaten and murdered for no more substantial reason than to satisfy a private grudge, to secure a man's job or his apartment, and to gratify a taste for sadism.' This was the revolution of the S.A. in power; but when Roehm came into conflict with the Army leadership, the S.A. was broken in the purge of 30 June 1934, in which Hitler murdered some of his oldest friends, and in exchange secured, a month later, the succession to Hindenburg from the Army very well satisfied with the events of that June weekend. There is no denying the ability with which he got the better of all his domestic opponents, and next of the statesmen on the international scene. They were feeble; they would not believe that anyone could act as Hitler did, time after time; and he had luck—his methods suited the circumstances. Still, the fact remains that under Hitler the German nation won victories and attained an extension of power not seen in Europe since the days of Napoleon, and far surpassing what it had achieved in the First World War; and that in so far as the leadership was concerned, diplomatic and military, the merit was mainly with Hitler himself. He and his story pose the insoluble enigma of success.

Hitler's mind was uncreative and unoriginal, and he 'seems to have been genuinely unaware of the extent of his unoriginality'. His appearance was unimpressive, 'plebeian through and through, with none of the physical characteristics of the racial superiority he was always invoking'; while in his coarse and curiously undistinguished face, the eyes alone attracted attention. His imagination, soaked in German neo-romanticism, produced a travesty of Wagner, Nietzsche, and Schopenhauer. Originality he achieved solely 'in the terrifying literal way in which he set to work to translate fantasy into reality', war and conquest having removed all restraint on him. 'The S.S. extermination squads,' writes Mr. Bullock, 'the *Einsatzkommandos*, with their gas-vans and death camps; the planned elimination of the Jewish race; the treatment of the Poles and Russians, the Slav *Untermenschen*—these ... were fruits of Hitler's imagination.' No generous ideas inspired the Nazi revolution whose only themes were domination and destruction. 'It is this emptiness, this lack of anything to justify the suffering he caused ... which makes Hitler both so repellent and so barren a figure.'

In the end megalomania wrought Hitler's own destruction. Suspicion of the expert, class-resentment against the Officer Corps, and a firm belief that he himself was endowed with more than ordinary gifts, made him assume the direction of war, even in detail. His 'unbounded confidence' in himself, of which he boasted, destroyed self-criticism and cut him off from reality. More and more, he shut himself up and 'lived in a private world of his own, from which the ugly facts of Germany's situation were excluded'. Finally he could no longer be persuaded to make a speech in public: he said he was waiting for a military success; Mr. Bullock suspects a deeper reason: 'Hitler's gifts as an orator had always depended on his flair for sensing what was in the minds of his audience. He no longer wanted to know what was in the minds of the German people.' And then, when his power had vanished and the enemy was closing in on him, nothing remained but a snarling, raving maniac, who in his quieter hours bored his companions with a monotonous repetition of reminiscences from his youth, and with 'anecdotes about his dog and his diet, interspersed with complaints about the stupidity and wickedness of the world'. At fifty-five he was an old man with ashen complexion and shuffling gait. 'It was no longer simply his left hand, but the whole left side of his body that trembled ...' writes General Guderian. 'He walked awkwardly, stooped more than ever, and his gestures were both jerky and slow. He had to have a chair pushed under him when he wished to sit down.' And another witness at a conference in Hitler's bunker, in February 1945: 'His head was slightly wobbling.... There was an indescribable flickering glow in his eyes, creating a fearsome and unnatural effect. His face and the parts around his eyes gave the impression of total exhaustion.' Yet at this, and at other conferences, he would shout at his Service chiefs his impossible demands and arbitrary decisions, treating them as pygmies who failed to rise to the level of his genius and vision, or cursing them for their cowardice, treachery, and incompetence: in the increasing vulgarity of his language, the Hitler

L

of the Vienna days was once more to the force. Amid the sufferings and defeat he had brought on Germany, he thought of himself as betrayed, by a people unworthy of their Führer. On 19 March 1945, he said to Speer, his Minister for Armaments and Munitions:

> If the war is to be lost, the nation also will perish. . . . There is no need to consider the basis even of a most primitive existence any longer. On the contrary, it is better to destroy even that, and to destroy it ourselves.

A crude fantasy of a Wagnerian 'Night of the Gods', farcical and ludicrous like all his fancies and ideas when he had no longer the power to inflict them as tragedy on millions of men. Yet his ghost and figure may work still further havoc. The relation of the Germans to him and what he stands for in their history, will deeply affect its further course.

'THE NEMESIS OF POWER'

THE PART played by the German Army in the politics of the Weimar Republic and of the Third Reich forms the central theme of Mr. John Wheeler-Bennett's new book *The Nemesis of Power*. It is the paradoxical story of maximum ascendancy attained by the army leaders under the Parliamentary Republic, and of gradual decline in status under Hitler; of the way in which they who despised the parliamentary régime and patronized the Nazis brought about their own downfall and humiliation.

The book links up with Mr. Wheeler-Bennett's previous three major works on contemporary history, *Hindenburg*, *Brest-Litovsk*, and *Munich*, and is his crowning achievement in that field: in it the *genre* which he has created appears in a matured and highly perfected form. Writers of contemporary history are usually either men who had a direct share in its making, or who had watched the scene from a distance: which gives their work an egocentric or an academic character. Mr. Wheeler-Bennett has intimately known many of the actors in the drama, and watched them at work, but without playing an active part of his own; and next he settled down to years of study of documentary evidence concerning the events he had witnessed, in a manner worthy of a master historian, keeping at the same time in close touch with men who from their own experience could help to elucidate and supplement such evidence. Impersonal in his work and yet supremely interested in his subject, alert and a good listener, he has the gift of eliciting information and critically incorporating it into his story. There is in him a touch of Boswell, and more than a touch of Horace Walpole who moved among the leading politicians but seldom had a political task to perform, and thus became the observer *par excellence*. Diplomacy or politics would have been for Mr. Wheeler-Bennett his obvious choice of a career; ill-health in his earlier years debarred him from either; and so he, too, settled down as an observer, where in the regular course he might have been a doer, with the limitations which action imposes. Circumstances determine our lives, but we shape our lives by what we make of circumstances.

The theme of Mr. Wheeler-Bennett's new book is crucial to the history of our time. When, on 7 May 1945, a representative of the German High Command signed the instrument of Unconditional Surrender, it was hoped that the German era in European history, so replete with disaster, had reached its term, and that the foremost aim of the Allies, repeatedly emphasized by their leaders, would be realized; Prussian militarism was to be destroyed along with the iniquities of National Socialism. The Prussian Army had enabled the Hohenzollerns and their servants to forge the bonds of German unity, the basis of German predominance in Europe. During the first world war the German High Command, under Hindenburg and Ludendorff, established its supremacy over the civilian government, and even over its own nominal Supreme Commander, the Emperor. When military defeat put an end to monarchical rule, the Army re-emerged under the Republic as the guardian of order and of national unity. Never was its independence and political power more pronounced than under the Weimar Republic; and it was even greater during the six years of the Socialist President Ebert than during the next eight years, when Hindenburg, premier soldier of the Reich, overshadowed the Army Command. The fear of Bolshevism at home, and the desire to see Germany's might re-established abroad, made the Army leaders into recognized arbiters of the internal affairs of the Reich and, to a great extent, of its foreign policy also.

In October 1918 Ludendorff hysterically cried out for an armistice and, to placate President Wilson, helped to stage a democratic transformation. The moderate Socialists, while making revolutionary gestures, frantically tried to shore up the imperial régime; they feared responsibility and they hated communism. Hoisted into power, Ebert, on the first night in the Chancellor's office, made a well-nigh symbolic discovery: on the table stood a telephone connecting him by a private and secret line with Army Headquarters. It rang: General Gröner, Ludendorff's successor, was speaking. Was the Government willing to protect Germany from anarchy and to restore order, he asked. Yes, it was. 'Then the High Command will maintain discipline in the Army and bring it peacefully home.' In a few sentences a pact was concluded between a defeated army and a tottering semi-revolutionary régime; and the Weimar Republic was doomed at birth. The Socialist Government helped to restore the authority of the Officer Corps; and when the troops, like victors, marched through the Brandenburger Tor with standards and music and arms, they were greeted by Ebert with the words: 'I salute you, who return unvanquished from the field of battle'. So saying, he unwittingly absolved the General Staff and indicted the revolution. The legend of the 'stab-in-the-back' was born.

Soon the General Staff was dictating to the Socialist Government. Ebert, bourgeois at heart and patriotic German, retained a deep respect for a Prussian Field-Marshal; Noske, Socialist Minister of Defence, purred when flattered by army officers. Polish incursions and Communist risings were apprehended; and with the Army practically disbanded, the High Command started raising from its wreckage Free Corps of 'politically reliable' adventurers and gangsters, the nuclei of future Nazi formations. Legalized by the Socialist Government, they crushed the Berlin Communists; and the National Assembly met to draft a constitution and conclude peace.

'In 1919, as in 1945', writes Mr. Wheeler-Bennett, 'no collective sense of war-guilt was evident among the German people', and the peace terms, however just, came as a shock to them. Ebert, inclining to rejection, consulted the military on the possibility of armed resistance. Their soundings yielded most discouraging results: the people were war-weary; the extreme left would rise, the Allies march in; the Officer Corps would be destroyed, and the name of Germany disappear from the map. The reply of the Army Command left no choice to Government and parliament; yet formally the decision to sign was made by the parliamentary ministers, henceforth the target of Nationalist hatred, abuse, and bullets.

The Kapp *Putsch* of March 1920, an attempt of the extreme Right and of rebel generals to seize power, was defeated by a general strike, while the Reichswehr under General von Seeckt remained neutral. And yet, once the *Putsch* was over, Ebert, to avoid chaos, had to renew with Seeckt the pact of November 1918; and when workers, armed during the *Putsch*, refused to disarm, they were ruthlessly put down by the Free Corps. Again, when during and after the Ruhr occupation revolutionary and separatist movements broke out in various parts of Germany, the government of the Reich was entrusted to Seeckt and the Reichswehr, the artificers and guardians of the German unitary state.

What mattered to Seeckt was the restoration of German power. Political strife being detrimental to discipline, he made the Reichswehr eschew sterile ambitions and adventures: aristocratic in character, ideologically linked up with the old Army, under him it kept aloof from current politics. Technically he made it a military microcosm capable of unlimited expansion. With an intake of a mere 8,000 a year, he could insist on high standards of physical and intellectual fitness. At one time there were 40,000 N.C.O.s among its statutory 96,000 'other ranks': this was to be an army not of mercenaries but of leaders. Seeckt envisaged the future war as one of movement, to be waged by comparatively small armies of high quality. The necessary equipment, denied to Germany by the peace treaty, he would obtain from Soviet Russia; for him and the Reichswehr she was the natural ally, France an implacable enemy, and Poland's very existence was intolerable: the Russo-German frontier of 1914 was to be restored. Close contact was secretly maintained with the Red General Staff; aircraft, motors, etc., were to be manufactured in Russia; tank and flying schools were established with German participation. New types of weapons were studied, and ordnance works in neutral countries were brought

under German control; in December 1925, the month of the
Locarno Agreements, Krupp acquired a controlling interest in
the great Bofors works in Sweden, to manufacture there the
latest patterns of heavy guns, anti-aircraft guns, and tanks.

Stresemann wished to conciliate the Western Powers in order
to expedite the end of Allied military occupation. His aim was
the same as Seeckt's: the restoration of the German *Machtstaat*.
From a study of the available evidence, Mr. Wheeler-Bennett
and the eminent American historian, Professor Sontag, have
reached the conclusion that Stresemann, holder of the Nobel
Peace Prize, was well-informed of Seeckt's policy and fully
aware of Germany's illegal rearmament, first in Russia and
later in Germany. A renewal of Germany's aggressive force was
well and truly secured, and had these men been able to complete their work, Germany's frontiers and dominance would
have been re-established and extended by a different version
either of Munich or of the Ribbentrop-Molotov treaty.

Ebert died in February 1925, and Hindenburg, in his seventy-
ninth year, became his successor. The President was now actual
Supreme Commander of the armed forces and his military
entourage started dabbling in politics—foremost, Kurt von
Schleicher, a brilliant staff officer with a passion for intrigue.
Seeckt resigned in October 1926. His period, writes Mr.
Wheeler-Bennett, 'had seen the German Army established as
the strongest single political factor within the State, the recognized guardian of the Reich; the Schleicher period saw the
descent of the Army into the arena of political intrigue, with a
consequent besmirching of its reputation and the ultimate
destruction of its authority'.

Schleicher is to Mr. Wheeler-Bennett 'the evil genius of the
later Weimar Period'. In time of parliamentary decay and political confusion a clever intriguer in the entourage of Hindenburg, that senile *faux bon homme*, could indeed do infinite
harm. Yet so far as the Reichswehr is concerned, can the blame
be squarely placed on his shoulders? Was Seeckt's political
aloofness ever sincere? Did not his attitude to revolt vary with
the quarter from which it came? By 1930, as Mr. Wheeler-
Bennett points out, both officers and the rank and file of the

Reichswehr were infected with Nazism. When, by order of Gröner, then Minister of Defence, three subalterns were prosecuted for Nazi propaganda, their Colonel, the later General Beck, leader of the conspiracy of 20 July 1944, defended them: 'The Reichswehr', he said, 'is told daily that it is an army of leaders. What is a young officer to understand by that?' A year later Seeckt himself appeared on Hitler's platform at the Harzburg Rally. And when, in April 1932, Gröner, the man with the cleanest record in that sordid period, tried to suppress the S.A. and the S.S., he was told by Schleicher that he 'no longer enjoyed the confidence of the Army'. They were dreaming 'of a martial state in which the masses, galvanized and inspired by modified National Socialism, would be directed and disciplined by the Army'.

In the early days of the Third Reich, the Army was a petted favourite, deferred to in all things; they, in turn, preserved impervious equanimity toward the ever-increasing horrors of Nazi terror and the moral record of the S.A. But within a year a situation was developing of supreme danger for the Army: while its guardian, Hindenburg, was rapidly declining, Röhm, at the head of 2,500,000 disgruntled Storm Troopers, demanded that the army should be merged with the Nazi para-military formations. Then a compact was concluded between Hitler and Blomberg, and unanimously accepted by the senior officers: the Army was to support Hitler for the presidency, and in return he undertook to put an end to the military claims of Röhm and the S.A. Hitler's part of the bargain was fulfilled in the Blood Purge of 30 June; but other disputes also were settled that day by murder. The upper ranks of the military hierarchy had been well aware of what was coming, and by permitting the butchery which rid them of rivals accepted the moral standards of the Third Reich. On 25 July followed the murder of Dollfuss. And when Hindenburg died on 1 August, and Hitler proclaimed himself Führer and Reich Chancellor, Blomberg, Fritsch, and Raeder, followed by all the armed forces, took an oath of personal fealty to him. They became Hitler's Army.

In March 1935 Hitler announced Germany's rearmament and introduced conscription, which filled the ranks with young

Nazis. A year later, against opposition from the military, he took what seemed a mad risk by marching into the Rhineland, and scored a victory over his hesitant generals: now the last remnant of respect vanished from his attitude towards them. Even within the Reich they ceased to be a serious political factor. They had been great while Socialist ministers reverently deferred to their judgement; they grew puny when roughly handled by Nazi toughs. On 5 November 1937, Hitler expounded to them his plans with regard to Austria and Czechoslovakia. Once more they were appalled at the risks he proposed to take. Still, it was not over basic issues but over Blomberg's marriage and the Fritsch scandal that, in January 1938, an acute crisis broke out among the top ranks of the German Army. For the first time they rose against the iniquities of the Gestapo because one of their own body was the victim. Even so their action was ill-concerted and ineffective; and interest in that disgusting and farcical story vanished when Hitler successfully invaded Austria.

Pastor Dietrich Bonhöffer, executed by the Nazis in April 1945, said in 1940, at the peak of Nazi successes: 'If we claim to be Christians, there is no room for expediency. Hitler is anti-Christ. Therefore we must go on with our work and eliminate him whether he be successful or not'. And Bonhöffer prayed for the defeat of Germany, for, said he, 'only in defeat can we atone for the terrible crimes we have committed against Europe and the world'. There were Germans who opposed Hitler on moral grounds, and honour must be done to their memory. But, writes Mr. Wheeler-Bennett, their number was 'small beyond belief in a nation of 80,000,000'. The opposition in the summer of 1938 was not against war but against the horrifying prospect of a war which Germany might not win. Accurate knowledge of Germany's weakness and an inaccurate evaluation of the strength and courage of the Powers opposed to her roused resistance to Hitler in military circles. Was there a serious plot against him, baulked by Chamberlain's journeys to Berchtesgaden and Munich? Mr. Wheeler-Bennett's examination of 'that carefully organized uprising which withered at the first touch of reality' discloses ineptitude in planning and fatal hesitancy in execution, and the rapidity with which the conspirators seized an excuse for their inaction is, he writes, 'at least an indication of their unreadiness'.

On that conspiracy, much publicized at the Nuremberg trials, followed a long, almost unbroken period of plotting, of amateurish efforts, of quasi-plans, and fanciful academic discussion: till at long last the approaching national disaster forced on the *coup* of 20 July 1944, again remarkable for ineptitude and hesitancy in execution. Mr. Wheeler-Bennett's analysis of the available mass of evidence enables the reader to see those conspiracies as one whole, and as part of the history of the German Officer Corps, or rather of its top-ranking circles. For while a majority of these, at one time or another, participated in conspiratorial talks, or at least were cognizant of them, nothing is known of a revolutionary ferment among junior officers or among the rank and file. Similarly support from the masses never entered into the calculations of plotters against Hitler. When in October 1939 the so-called 'X-report', alleging that the British Government were ready to conclude peace with a non-Nazi Government on terms favourable to Germany, was shown by General Thomas to Brauchitsch, then Commander-in-Chief of the German Army, he took no action against the conspirators nor against Hitler either.

> I could have had Hitler arrested easily (he said to one of the conspirators after the war)... But... why should I have taken such action? It would have been action against the German people... The German people were all for Hitler. And they had good reason to be, particularly the working man. Nobody had ever done so much to raise their standards of living as Hitler.

There was a revolt of starving working men in Eastern Germany in June 1953, but when well fed by Hitler, at other people's expense, they had no thought of rising. Apparently revolutionaries, at least in Germany, march like armies on their stomachs, except that theirs have to be empty.

Who then were these German resisters to Hitler? Foremost generals, diplomats, and high civil servants opposed to him on technical and professional grounds: they agreed with the aims of his foreign policy, and at each stage wished to consolidate the gains secured by him, but feared that his methods would engulf Germany in fresh disaster. Hence the spirit of resistance in them rose or dropped in accordance with the dangers he incurred or the successes he achieved. Moral disapproval was at best a contributory factor, usually weak, or it was altogether absent: before Hitler plunged into foreign adventures most of these men had readily served him, undeterred by his crimes. In November 1939, one of the military chiefs thus defined his attitude toward revolt against Hitler: 'The military situation of Germany', he said, 'particularly on account of the pact of non-aggression with Russia, is such that a breach of my oath to the Führer could not possibly be justified.' Conscience determined by fine calculations makes neither effective rebels nor heroes.

In fact these conspiracies were mostly of the 'palace revolution' type, and leading plotters at times considered replacing Hitler by Göring, or even by Himmler. When in 1943 Field-Marshal von Bock, whose Headquarters in Russia were the operational centre of conspiracy, declared that he would not join any plot unless Himmler was in it, an attempt was made to gain Himmler's co-operation. Popitz, Prussian Minister of Finance, conveyed to him some of the aims of the plotters, and claimed to have found him not averse in principle: a common friend was allowed to meet Allied Intelligence officers in Switzerland, and only when a relevant message from an Allied agency was decoded by German rivals of Himmler, did he disavow and intern that friend. That such talks should have been possible illustrates conditions in both German camps and the *Realpolitik* of the German 'resistance' movement. But foresight in men without backbone, unsupported as it is by moral convictions or passion, cannot engender determined revolutionary action. Hence the ineffectiveness of the one big plot, that of 20 July 1944.

As the Russian armies were pressing on and German cities were reduced to rubble by Anglo-American bombing, a sense of urgency arose among the plotters. Once rid of Hitler they counted on being able to negotiate, and perhaps to start a bidding-match between the Anglo-Saxon Powers and Soviet Russia. Still, the only way to eliminate Hitler satisfactorily was to kill him. Many generals claimed to be bound by their oath of allegiance to obey Hitler, though apparently not to protect him from murder: was this an involution of the German conscience unfathomable to non-Germans, or disguised fear of the living Hitler? Either way it proved decisive on 20 July. But why did the many plots against his life all fail? Why did a conspiracy of unequalled dimensions, with exceptional facilities and means, fail to achieve in seven years what in other countries is often done by groups of insignificant conspirators? Because most of the would-be German assassins called off at the last moment; while two attempts which were carried through mark a new technique in tyrannicide: murder by indirect fire, *in absentia*. Had Count Stauffenburg, instead of leaving behind a time bomb, handled it himself, he would have died twelve hours earlier than he did, but Hitler would have died with him. There is cogency in the argument of Erich Kordt, who himself claims to have planned in 1939 Hitler's assassination, but admits to having dropped the idea 'with suspicious speed'. 'Few', he writes, 'are prepared to strive for an end and renounce seeing it accomplished'; and 'all watchfulness... can protect a tyrant only against those who mean to witness the sequel...'. The plotters of 20 July were to witness the horrible sequel of an attempt that failed.

Time after time before the war Hitler had proved right and his generals had proved wrong; but over questions of policy and not of strategy. During the war even in these his judgement repeatedly triumphed over theirs: they refused to operate the occupation of Denmark and Norway, being convinced that it would fail; and they did not believe that a break-through in France was possible. Their prestige and authority consequently dwindled, while the disdainful insolence and ruthless brutality with which Hitler treated them grew beyond bounds. After 20 July 1944, he could give vent to long suppressed feelings: he had the aristocratic military caste in the hollow of his hand. 'You dirty old man', shouted the Nazi judge Freisler at an ex-Field-Marshal; 'You are a filthy rascal', at another officer.

They, for their part, made 'pitiable attempts to excuse themselves', and 'not one of them', writes Mr. Wheeler-Bennett, 'could muster up the strength of will to interrupt the flow of Freisler's obscene rhetoric and to make it clear . . . why they stood in the dock and why they would shortly die'. 'It is my wish that they be hanged like cattle', decreed Hitler; and they were hanged on meat hooks screwed into the ceiling.

And those not directly implicated in the plot? The failure of a few 'to carry out what all had known to be necessary' left the Officer Corps fawning and frightened. They were ordered to give in future the Hitler salute, and to declare their adherence to National Socialism. 'None resigned, none resisted'. 'The Nemesis of Power' had overtaken the once-proud Officer Corps.